MW01043354

THE ABCs OF ETHICS

ALSO BY
MICHAEL L. BUCKNER

Athletics Investigation Handbook: A Guide for Institutions and Involved Parties During the NCAA Enforcement Process

THE ABCs OF ETHICS

A Resource for Leaders, Managers, and Professionals

MICHAEL L. BUCKNER

iUniverse, Inc.
New York   Bloomington

The ABCs of Ethics
A Resource for Leaders, Managers, and Professionals

Copyright © 2010 Michael L. Buckner

All rights reserved. No part of this book may be used or reproduced by any means, graphic, electronic, or mechanical, including photocopying, recording, taping or by any information storage retrieval system without the written permission of the publisher except in the case of brief quotations embodied in critical articles and reviews.

iUniverse books may be ordered through booksellers or by contacting:

iUniverse Star
an iUniverse, Inc. imprint

iUniverse
1663 Liberty Drive
Bloomington, IN 47403
www.iuniverse.com
1-800-Authors (1-800-288-4677)

Because of the dynamic nature of the Internet, any Web addresses or links contained in this book may have changed since publication and may no longer be valid. The views expressed in this work are solely those of the author and do not necessarily reflect the views of the publisher, and the publisher hereby disclaims any responsibility for them.

ISBN: 978-1-935278-49-8(pbk)
ISBN: 978-1-935278-50-4(ebk)

Printed in the United States of America

Library of Congress Control Number: 2009911851

iUniverse rev. date: 2/12/2010

For people who acknowledge their imperfections, yet refuse to surrender in the ongoing battle to improve themselves, as well as their surroundings.

CONTENTS

ACKNOWLEDGMENTS

This project would not have been possible without the love, support, and encouragement of my wife, Shawn, my parents, and my uncle, Adam, all of whom provided me with excellent examples of ethical behavior. Also, I wish to thank the many gifted professionals who labored to evaluate and edit this work.

WHAT "ETHICS" STANDS FOR

E: Earn the respect of others by being respectful.

T: Treat others as you would want people to treat you and your loved ones.

H: Honor all promises and commitments.

I: Increase your perspective of integrity, honesty, commitment, and trust every day.

C: Care about yourself while balancing the needs of others.

S: Share with others.

PREFACE

The ABCs of Ethics is designed for leaders, managers, professionals, students, and other persons interested in improving ethical behavior within themselves, inside organizations, and throughout society. This project was initiated to address a fundamental question impacting ethical behavior in our society: what does it mean to be ethical? This question surfaces on a regular basis in my professional career and personal life. In particular, I encounter people who refuse (or do not know how) to apply an appropriate ethical standard to their behavior. Clients also request my assistance to provide solutions to problems that demand reliance on ethical standards.

As a result, over the course of my career as a lawyer, private investigator, consultant, and seminar/workshop presenter, I have come to realize that ethics are not mere codes, rules, regulations, and laws. Instead, as aptly described by Claire Andre and Manuel Velasquez in an article for *Issues in Ethics*, "ethics refers to well based standards of right and wrong that prescribe what humans ought to do, usually in terms of rights, obligations, benefits to society, fairness, or specific virtues" and "to the study and development of one's ethical standards."[1]

Accordingly, *The ABCs of Ethics* presents stories, anecdotes, examples, questions, and other information using the framework of the English alphabet to facilitate discussion, reflection, and analysis about the meaning of ethics. I researched a variety of books, articles, journals, research projects, and Internet sources to provide a foundation for an easy-to-read discussion of ethical concepts. In addition, I conducted interviews with administrators at major intercollegiate athletics programs. The interviews produced insightful information on how well-run athletics programs rely on ethical behavior to produce results on the field and in the classroom. Thus, the practical insight obtained from my interviews with leading athletics administrators can be applied by persons in any field or profession. I also relied on my experiences as an attorney, private investigator, consultant, and seminar/workshop presenter in preparing the text.

It is my hope that this work will create a better understanding of what type of behavior should be tolerated within organizations and by individuals.

The ABCs of Ethics can be assigned as the main resource for ethics education and training sessions or as a supplemental text for an ethics course. *The ABCs of Ethics* also can be used as a resource for personal study and reflection.

INTRODUCTION

October 30, 2005, was an exciting occasion for the thousands of runners and walkers who converged on the Washington, DC, area to compete in the Marine Corps Marathon. JeansMarines, a non-profit organization "whose mission is to lead women toward a mighty goal: to run or walk a marathon,"[2] was one of several organizations with participants in the 26.2-mile event. During the race, several JeansMarines runners and walkers used a shortcut near the fifteen-mile mark and, subsequently, rejoined the marathon course near the twenty-mile mark. According to news reports, JeansMarines founder Dr. Jean Marmoreo advised her slower runners and walkers to use the short-cut to reach the twenty-mile mark prior to the marathon's mandatory six-hour cutoff time. (Most marathons open parts of the course to vehicular traffic after a certain period.) The runners and walkers used the shortcut, concluded the remaining 6.2 miles of the marathon, and received "finisher" medals for completing the race. However, eyewitnesses notified race officials of the course deviation used by the participants. JeansMarines later admitted to the course deviation. The organization also requested that the runners and walkers who used the shortcut return their finisher medals.[3]

The marathon community, which depends on self-regulation during competitions, engaged in a spirited debate on the ethics of the shortcut. On discussion boards and blogs, marathoners, runners, walkers, and others pondered whether the participants committed an egregious error or a harmless mistake.[4] The majority of respondents labeled the situation an example of cheating. However, a minority believed that the unfairness of a course cut-off time and the admirable goal of finishing a long-distance race justified the shortcut.

The lively discussion and lessons learned concerning the marathon shortcut are relevant guidance for leaders, managers, professionals, students, athletes, and others who seek to understand the notion of ethics. The organization Character Unlimited, which provides character development training in the workplace, in schools, and for juvenile justice systems, defines ethics as "moral rights and wrongs" that "transcend culture, ethnicity, and are relevant to all socioeconomic conditions."[5] Numerous organizations have spent precious resources retaining consultants and experts to develop grand vision and mission statements, ethics codes, and compliance programs. These organizations hope that written pronouncements are the "magic pill" that will eliminate ethical missteps and bolster public confidence. For example, a lawyer cannot sustain a law practice if clients cannot rely on his or her integrity and character. Further, a person will more likely invest in a corporation without ethical incidents.

However, codes of ethics are mere written words. Codes do not ensure ethical behavior. Codes cannot guide employees when faced with everyday ethical dilemmas. In fact, according to a February 21, 2002, ABC News report by Michael S. Jones, some of the reasons people act unethically in the workplace include: rationalization, bad role models in the organization, peer pressure, difficulty in defining what is "ethical behavior," organizational culture, and pressure from superiors.[6] Thus, a shift in the way of thinking on an organizational and personal level is necessary to address the reasons for unethical behavior. Specifically, ethical behavior can be encouraged, developed, and embraced through an organizational and personal culture of doing what is right and fair in every decision. What does that lofty premise mean? I believe James P. Owen in his book *Cowboy Ethics: What Wall Street Can Learn from the Code of the West* correctly described the concept when summarizing a May 2004 speech by then Securities and Exchange Commission chairman William H. Donaldson to the National Association of Securities Dealers:

> It means instilling "a company-wide commitment to do the right thing, this time and every time" so that ethical behavior becomes "the core of the company's essential DNA" and "is shared by every employee." It means a firm's leaders should have the "courage and commitment" to question whether a particular practice is truly ethical or truly in the best interests of clients and customers, no matter what the layers say. It means that "customers always come before the balance sheet and not the other way around."[7]

This book seeks to assist persons with developing or improving on an organizational or personal commitment "to do the right thing." As such, I used the English alphabet as a convenient means to organize the book's message. Each chapter is dedicated to a letter of the alphabet. The chapter contains a message connected to a word, or a phrase using a word, that begins with the letter. Further, each chapter ends with questions for self-reflection or additional study. The questions are designed to assist the reader with enhancing his or her own understanding of ethics, as well as what ethics means to his or her organization.

Improvement in organizational and personal ethical behavior starts with the individual. It is my hope that this book can be one of several devices you use to begin the lifelong journey to understanding ethics.

ETHICAL INSIGHT FROM VARIOUS SOURCES OF WISDOM

An organization that lacks the attention to details with regards to its compliance can create a weaker ethical organization.

—Debra Gore-Mann, director of athletics at the University of San Francisco

In law a man is guilty when he violates the rights of others. In ethics he is guilty if he only thinks of doing so.

—Immanuel Kant, philosopher

Professional ethics depends mainly on constant vigilance, on sustained discretion and prudence, and on wisdom, rather than on certain set rules.

—Tibor R. Machan, professor emeritus, department of philosophy, Auburn University

NOTE ON THE QUESTIONS
FOR REFLECTION OR
FURTHER STUDY

Each chapter ends with at least two questions for self-reflection or additional study. The questions are designed to assist the reader with enhancing his or her own understanding of ethics, as well as what ethics means to his or her organization. Interested readers are invited to submit responses to the author via e-mail (mbuckner@michaelbucknerlaw.com). The responses will be compiled and published in newsletters and other resources so that others can use the collective insight and wisdom to further their study of ethical behavior.

CHAPTER 1: A
ACTION SPEAKS LOUDER
THAN WORDS

Action speaks louder than words but not nearly as often.

—Mark Twain

The superior man is modest in his speech, but exceeds in his actions.

—Confucius

Content yourself with doing, leave the talking to others.

—Baltasar Gracián

When I began practicing law, I was horrified to learn that a sizeable number of employment relationships between coaches and universities were consummated through a handshake or through a sparsely worded letter agreement. As a lawyer employed at a large corporate law firm, this business practice appeared old-fashioned and ripe for serious legal problems. I was accustomed to drafting, editing, and litigating contracts and agreements spanning numerous—and sometimes hundreds of—pages. I also conducted seminars and workshops during which I advised colleges and universities to draft comprehensive employment agreements. Over the years, more colleges and universities began finalizing employment relationships with coaches of athletics teams in well-drafted, detailed, and complex agreements. Thus, the days of the handshake deal are coming to a close. The lawyers (who are compensated for the work), the employers (who hope all contingencies have been addressed in the agreement), and the employees (who trust their interests have been protected) stand to benefit. Or do they?

Unfortunately, what I failed to appreciate during my early years of law practice is the basis for the handshake deal and the simple letter agreement. In the "old days," parties usually said what they meant. F. David Peat, cofounder of the Pari Center for New Learning, recounted: "When, in the late 17th

Century, bankers, merchants and shippers met in Edward Lloyd's Coffee House they carried out their transactions based on the principle of 'my word is my bond.' Indeed in English law a verbal agreement, sealed by a handshake, was legally binding, the written contract being only a memorandum of what had been agreed upon by both parties." Most importantly, Peat noted the seventeenth century economic system was "based on three invisible pillars of Trust, Honesty and Respect, ethical principles that were taken for granted in that period."[8] Thus, the actions of each party became more important than what was said or written down. Accordingly, history teaches us that legal documents are not and cannot be the only glue holding together relationships. Instead, any professional and personal interaction should be built on a strong ethical foundation of trust, honesty, and respect.

Questions for Reflection or Further Study

1. When was the last time you concluded a deal or negotiation with only a handshake or oral promise? Why was a written contract not used?

2. Why do you think our society relies on complex contracts to govern business, professional, and personal relationships?

3. Could you or your organization maintain a business, professional, or personal relationship without a complex contract? If yes, list the particular circumstances.

CHAPTER 2: B
BENEFICENCE

Principles of beneficence require us to promote the good.

—Liam B. Murphy

The University of Miami School of Medicine's Privacy/Data Protection Project describes *beneficence* as the notion that we should assist others to advance their vital and legal interests "as those persons understand them (respecting autonomy) or as we conceive them (paternalism)." Further, under the principle of beneficence, a person's "failure to increase the good of others when one is knowingly in a position to do so is morally wrong."[9] We should use the principle of beneficence in our professional career and personal life. Ultimately, beneficence produces a benefit to the organization, as well as to the persons who observe the practice. The most important benefits include client/customer satisfaction, professional success, and financial profit. An organization can receive a tangible benefit from applying beneficent behavior in behavior and decision-making.

For example, one beneficent application in business is the practice of open-book management. Professor of strategic management and philosophy Norman E. Bowie argues in *Companion to Business Ethics* that open-book management, which "was developed by Jack Stack at the Springfield Manufacturing Company," involves management providing "all employees [with] all the financial information about the company on a regular frequent basis." Thus, under open-book management, "with complete information and the proper incentive, employees behave responsibly without the necessity of layers of supervision." Further, open-book management addresses "the asymmetrical information that managers possess, a situation that promotes abuse of power and deception." Open book management also promotes "employee self-respect." For instance, if a firm, which practiced open-book management, "faced a situation that might involve the layoff of employees, everyone in the firm would have access to the same information." Bowie concludes "deception would be very difficult in such circumstances" and "suspicion would be less and, as a result, cooperative efforts to address the problem would be more likely." For a real world example, Bowie describes the "decision of the Marriott Corporation to hire welfare recipients" as one way of "honoring its obligation to realize profits and its obligation of beneficence."[10]

Questions for Reflection or Further Study

1. What are ways your organization promotes the principle of beneficence?

_____

_____

_____

_____

_____

2. Should competitors (in the marketplace, sports, or other areas of competition) adhere to the principle of beneficence? Explain your rationale.

_____

_____

_____

_____

_____

CHAPTER 3: C
CHARACTER DEVELOPMENT

Character is like a tree and reputation like its shadow. The shadow is what we think of it; the tree is the real thing.

—Abraham Lincoln

Character is not reflected by what we say, or even by what we intend, it is a reflection of what we do.

—Anonymous

Character is an important aspect of ethics. The organization Character Unlimited, which provides character development training in the workplace, in schools, and for juvenile justice systems, defines *character* as the "action you take to carry out the values, ethics and morals that you believe in."[11] The organization also notes that character is "Who you are and what you do when no one is looking." Likewise, *character development*, as described by The Ethics Resource Center, is "the long-term process of helping individuals develop knowledge of, motivation to, and practices of living by a set of ethical standards."[12] Thus, the development of character influences our ability to adhere to ethical standards.

Indeed, the pursuit of character development is important for individuals to undertake for professional and personal reasons. For this reason, teaching character development should be a component of an organization's education and training program. Character development is important for any organization because the organization is a collection of individuals. Each individual makes his or her own decisions about how to act or behave on behalf of the organization. Further, each individual encounters opportunities to make the organization a more or less ethical place. Thus, a person's decisions, behavior, and actions can powerfully impact others inside and outside the organization. Accordingly, an organization guarantees a positive outcome from blending character development and organizational values in a proactive ethics education and training program.

For instance, the success of Super Bowl XLI-winning head football coach Tony Dungy, then of the National Football League Indianapolis Colts, illustrates how organizations succeed when managers use character development to lead.[13] Conversely, the ethical hurdles faced by Enron Corporation points to a vacuum of character development (among other things).[14]

Questions for Reflection or Further Study

1. How do you carry out the ideas or concepts (e.g., values, ethics, morals) you believe in?

_____

_____

_____

_____

2. What do you do "when no one is looking" that is not consistent with how you carry out the ideas or concepts you believe in? Explain the reasons for the inconsistency.

_____

_____

_____

_____

3. Does your organization provide character development education and training? Why or why not?

_____

_____

_____

_____

4. What decisions or actions do persons in your organization make on a daily basis that are inconsistent with your belief system? Do you believe those persons' decisions or actions are unethical? Explain your rationale.

_____

_____

_____

_____

CHAPTER 4: D
DUE DILIGENCE

Diligence is the mother of good fortune, and idleness, its opposite, never led to good intention's goal.

—Miguel de Cervantes

The pursuit of attaining and maintaining high ethical standards is an ongoing process. Thus, an organization, as well as its members, can utilize a continual due diligence process to measure its ethical fitness and enhance compliance with its stated values.

Merriam-Webster's Dictionary defines *diligence* as "the attention and care legally expected or required of a person (as a party to a contract)." The nonprofit community organization Crossroads Programs, Inc., an organization pursuing ethical enhancement for itself, as well as its employees, exercises due diligence by implementing a code of ethics, encouraging dialogue, developing leadership, improving human resources, and enhancing systems. These five keys coexist in several organizations that espoused the highest ethical behavior.[15]

For example, making an ethical decision takes several steps—gathering facts, analyzing dilemmas, building moral arguments, and applying resolution principles. But none of them matters much without a crucial first step: recognizing that the issue at hand is in fact an ethical issue. Consider the ethical and legal issues produced during the Cendant scandal, which surfaced in 1998. It could be argued that the ethical collapse of Cendant occurred due to lack of due diligence. Cendant was created when Henry Silverman, leader of the Hospitality Franchise Systems (HFS)—which acquired the Ramada and Holiday Inn franchise systems, as well as Days Inns, Super 8 Motels, Century 21, Coldwell Banker, Travelodge, and Avis—merged HFS with CUC International, a direct-marketing firm with Walter Forbes at the helm. The merger produced a new company called Cendant with Silverman as chief executive officer and Forbes as board chairman. Cendant's stock price eventually rose to an all-time high of over $41. However, on April 15, 1998, the company reported the former CUC was involved in "accounting irregularities." Cendant's stock tumbled dramatically (with loses of approximately $14 billion) in response to the April 15 announcement. Forbes argues he did not know of the irregularities. It appeared on the surface that due diligence failed Cendant and its investors. But according to Rushworth Kidder in a commentary that appeared in the August 10, 1998, issue of *Ethics Newsline*, due diligence is "not something you do late in the game, when all you're looking at are the numbers. It's something much bigger than numbers, something you do up front when you first assess the nature of the people you're working with." Kidder advises that due diligence includes the use of "a conceptual framework for measuring the ethical fiber of potential partners, be they individuals or organizations."[16] The lesson from Cendant is that although deceitful persons can make due diligence difficult, it is not impossible.

Questions for Reflection or Further Study

1. Does your organization possess a current code of ethics that addresses typical ethical problems or predicaments in its industry? If yes, how has the information assisted you professionally and personally?

_____

_____

_____

_____

_____

2. Can questions of ethics be discussed in your organization freely or directed to a specific ethics officer or confidential source? If yes, does this encourage more ethical behavior in the organization?

_____

_____

_____

_____

_____

3. Does your organization's practices, decision-making, and actions consistently reflect its code of ethics or conduct? If no, describe instances when it does not, as well as the reasons for the inconsistency.

_____

_____

_____

_____

_____

CHAPTER 5: E
EGOISM

People wrapped up in themselves make very small packages.

—Anonymous

It can be argued that an organization or person only makes decisions that benefit the organization or person. This phenomenon can be described as *egoism*. Egoism is contrasted with the theory of altruism, which is defined as unselfish regard for or devotion to the welfare of others. Egoism, according to Wofford College philosophy professor Charles D. Kay, is a "theory of ethics that sets as its goal the benefit, pleasure, or greatest good of oneself alone."[17] The theory of egoism, as described by the University of Miami School of Medicine's Privacy/Data Protection Project, suggests a person's choices do or should "involve self-promotion as their sole objective."[18] In other words, egoism contends a person's "self" is or should be the motivation, as well as the goal, of his or her actions. An egoist also is someone who places his or her own self-interest above any other consideration. (Egoism should be distinguished from *egotism*, which *Merriam-Webster's Dictionary* defines as "a doctrine that individual self-interest is the valid end of all actions" or "excessive concern for oneself with or without exaggerated feelings of self-importance.")

Egoism includes several variations. For example, the Privacy/Data Protection Project describes one version of the theory, *psychological egoism*, as "the descriptive version, contending that people usually do what is in their self-interest." This theory argues a person "psychologically cannot ever act voluntarily against what" the person believes to be in his or her "best interest."[19] Thus, an altruistic, selfless, or philanthropic act is viewed as always promoting a person's long-run self-interest. Likewise, the behavior of a person who is free to act without constraint (e.g., free will) will always be consistent with his or her desires, preferences, and needs. As a result, it is important to understand the influence of egoism in organizational decision-making and personal behavior.

However, can an organization or individual act ethically and still be an egoist? According to John Collins in a *Business Horizons* article, an egoist does not have a role in an ethical organization. Collins explains that an "ethical egoist" is an employee that "may sometimes choose to act unethically" because he or she believes "that unethical conduct is in their own self-interest." In response, Collins recommends "that employees must be encouraged to bring their ethics to work."[20]

One example of an egoist is supplied by Stephen Parrish in his review of Tara Smith's *Viable Values: A Study of Life as the Root and Reward of Morality*:

> If it is in your best interest to obtain ten million dollars, and a practically risk-free opportunity to embezzle that much money arises, then on egoistic principles, where every ethical action is governed by what is best for the individual, it would seem that the ethical thing to do would be to embezzle. And this seems obviously wrong.[21]

Similarly, the story of Andrew Speaker provides a real-life illustration of Parrish's description of an egoist. Speaker, an Atlanta lawyer, flew on several airplanes in May 2007 while infected with what was then believed to be a dangerous form of tuberculosis (TB). According to media reports, Speaker "knew he had TB when he flew from Atlanta to Europe in mid-May for his wedding and honeymoon, but that he did not find out until he was already in Rome that it was an 'extensively drug-resistant' strain" of the disease. However, Speaker, who received "warnings from federal health officials not to board another long flight," used commercial airline flights to travel home for treatment. Despite placing fellow passengers at risk for contracting TB, Speaker later explained that he feared he would not survive if he stayed in Europe.[22]

Questions for Reflection or Further Study

1. Would you describe yourself as following the theory of egoism or altruism? Explain your rationale.

_____

_____

_____

_____

2. Who or what should be the beneficiary of a person's actions?

_____

_____

_____

_____

3. Is it possible for a person to act only according to his or her own interests without regard for another person's interests? Explain your rationale.

_____

_____

_____

_____

4. Is it possible for a person to act for another person in complete disregard for his or her own interests? Explain your rationale.

_____

_____

_____

_____

5. Can an organization effectively pursue its goals using the theory of egoism as the only basis for its ethical standards? Explain your rationale.

_____

_____

_____

_____

_____

CHAPTER 6: F
FINISHING WHAT YOU START

Obstacles don't have to stop you. If you run into a wall, don't turn around and give up. Figure out how to climb it, go through it, or work around it.

—Michael Jordan

Our energy is in proportion to the resistance it meets. We attempt nothing great but from a sense of the difficulties we have to encounter, we persevere in nothing great but from a pride in overcoming them.

—William Hazlitt

Fall seven times. Stand up eight.

—Japanese proverb

Completing projects or tasks can be a challenge even for the most studious person. The complexities of life, unforeseen hurdles, unexpected challenges, and lack of motivation can contribute to the feeling of wanting to give up. People in such positions oftentimes do not know what to do next. In fact, all of us, from the least successful to the most motivated person, have at least one area in our lives that remains unresolved. However, unsettled or unresolved projects, issues, or promises create situations when other persons (or yourself) are let down. Naturally, we expect everyone to finish what they start. For example, in *Cowboy Ethics: What Wall Street Can Learn from the Code of the West,* author James P. Owen explains that expectation was well-established in the old American West:

Cowboys hated quitters. They hated whining and complaining almost as much because those things had the stench of quitting. On a trail drive, it was when things got roughest that every hand was expected to give his all.[23]

The key to keeping on track and completing what needs to be done is to address the common routine when any of us fail to complete a project or keep a promise: a person starts a new project with excitement and optimism; challenges arise; a person procrastinates and postpones as his or her passion decreases. Challenges come in all shapes and sizes, from internal (e.g., fear, laziness) and external (e.g., transportation delays, technology problems) sources. However, the challenges most of us face are merely a test. Thus, whenever you come across a hurdle in your path, the key is to increase speed, proceed with skill, and negotiate the obstacle. The most successful and ethical people understand two things: there are no insurmountable barriers and a solution exists to every problem (we may not like the most reasonable or logical solution available, but one does exist). More often than not, you will not find a hurdle, but a paper barrier disguised to discourage you from attempting to overcome it. It is incumbent for each of us to understand, recognize, and improve our abilities to follow through on a project or a promise. For when we begin a project or make a promise, other people are relying on the expected results. Thus, when we do not finish what we start, we fail to live up to the promises announced or communicated at the start.

For example, as a lawyer and private investigator, I have an "ethical obligation to be loyal" to my clients, which is "closely related to the concept of promise-keeping." According to ethics writer Bruce Weinstein in a January 31, 2007, *Business Week* article, the word "professional" is derived from a Latin word that means "to make a public declaration." Thus, when I obtained my professional licenses, I publicly declared to devote my "knowledge or skills to the benefit of others." In other words, as a professional, my "primary mission is not to enrich" myself. Instead, I pledged to fulfill a client's expectation that I will provide recommendations that are based on the client's best interests and not mine.[24]

Questions for Reflection or Further Study

1. What are your most fulfilling moments in your life (professional and personal)? Did you experience any challenges prior to the moment of fulfillment? If yes, how did you overcome the challenges?

_____

_____

_____

_____

_____

2. List the instances in which you did not complete or finish a project or keep a promise? What were the reasons for not finishing what you started? Did your inability to complete a project or keep a promise impose undue hardship on yourself or other persons?

_____

_____

_____

_____

_____

CHAPTER 7: G
GRAY AREAS

Next time I am tempted to call something an ethical gray area, I will stop first and take stock. Is it really gray, or is that a cop-out because I am unwilling to go to the effort of discerning the actual blackness or whiteness?

—Wally Kroeker

All persons can maintain an ethical approach to decision making by avoiding *gray areas*. Deon Melchior, editor and publisher of *Article Click*, describes a gray area as "usually pertain[ing] to something unclear, something that can be looked at in different ways or that can be identified by different categories."[25] Princeton University's *WordNet* defines a gray area an "an intermediate area; a topic that is not clearly one thing or the other."[26] However, Charles E. Watson, author of *What Smart People Do When Dumb Things Happen at Work*, opines that "gray areas usually become the justification for what you should not be doing." He also observes that successful leaders avoid gray areas through acknowledging "the existence of right and wrong." As a result, employees will know that certain practices will not be tolerated. Most importantly, he notes a leader's refusal to deal in gray areas provides employees with "a clear understanding" of what are "the boundaries of acceptable behavior."[27]

The leaders and organizations with the highest ethical standards operate without a gray area. For example, Christians learn "that no lie is of the truth" and "that there is no possible harmony between a lie and the truth." In fact, Pastor Ray C. Stedman opines "that there are no gray areas in life; that a thing is either black (a lie) or it is white (the truth), and there are no gray areas, though there may be a mingling of black with white." Stedman's explanation suggests ethical people have "an ability to exercise moral judgment to distinguish right from wrong."[28]

For example, if a colleague, customer, supplier, friend, or other person provides us with valuable information without requesting confidentiality from us, should we feel free to use that information in any manner we see fit? The answer to this question lies in the response to a second question: What does the person who provided the information expect us to do with it? The ethics office at Texas Instruments Corporation, in response to a similar hypothetical, emphasized that the "key is to understand and to meet those expectations and this often requires us to actively seek them out." According to the Texas Instrument ethics office, a gray area does not exist because the expectations can be fleshed out by asking questions before the use of the information.[29] Likewise, we can avoid the ethical complexities created by operating in gray areas by identifying right and wrong, exploring our duties and responsibilities, understanding the expectations of others, and, most importantly, treating others how we would like to be treated.

Questions for Reflection or Further Study

1. Is it acceptable in our society to operate within the gray area? If yes, when?

_____

_____

_____

_____

_____

2. Does your organization provide a clear understanding of the boundaries of acceptable behavior?

_____

_____

_____

_____

_____

3. Have you ever been requested or directed to undertake an action that you believed fell in a gray area? If yes, what was the outcome?

_____

_____

_____

_____

_____

4. Have you been on the receiving end of a decision that was in the gray area? Would you have made the same decision if you were in the same position? Explain your rationale.

_____

_____

_____

_____

_____

CHAPTER 8: H
HONESTY AND HONOR

Honor and profit lie not in one sack.

—George Herbert

Honesty's the best policy.

—Cervantes

He has honor if he holds himself to an ideal of conduct though it is inconvenient, unprofitable, or dangerous to do so.

—Walter Lippman

An honest Man will receive neither Money nor Praise, that is not his Due.

—Benjamin Franklin

Every person embraces a certain characteristic over others. I cherish two traits above all others: honesty and honor. I am not alone. Some cultures place great importance on honesty and honor. For the ancient Romans, honor was so important that suicide was considered an appropriate means to defend a person's reputation. In fact, Drs. Leonardo Tondo and Ross J. Baldessarini, in a *Medscape Today* article, describe suicide as "not uncommon" in ancient Rome and said that it "was sometimes considered honorable among civic leaders and intellectuals." They note the great Roman senator and orator Marcus Tullius Cicero "generally condemned suicide, but accepted it as an act of heroism, self-sacrifice, or defense of honor."[30] I am not arguing that suicide is appropriate behavior, but ancient Rome's use of suicide in limited circumstances illustrates the significance of honor and honesty to some cultures.

Honor and honesty are important characteristics in professional and personal dealings. Indeed, organizations or people that fail, or neglect, to embrace ethical values will attract clients, customers, vendors, suppliers, and friends that share a similar distain for such values. Thus, an organization that identifies any way to cheat clients, customers, vendors, or suppliers eventually will be forced to deal with only those parties who are cheaters themselves. Each instance will result in the parties facing the consequence of *mutual attraction.* Namely, unethical organizations and persons attract one another. As a result, parties in such relationships will delay payment, use contractual language, and identify other ways to reduce their exposure to the unethical behavior of the other. The end result is two parties looking to outwit each other (albeit legally) instead of pursuing a mutual beneficial and satisfactory relationship. The scandal involving energy company Enron Corporation and accounting firm Arthur Anderson LLP is one example of two organizations that shared a disregard for ethical standards or practices. Enron was investigated by the federal government for illegal accounting practices. In January 2002, the government began a probe into Arthur Anderson, which provided accounting and consulting services for Enron. The federal inquiry revealed Andersen "deliberately destroyed crucial documents relating to Enron during October-November 2001." We can learn from Enron and Arthur Anderson's example by avoiding a mutual attraction that revolves around a disregard of honesty and honor.[31]

Questions for Reflection or Further Study

1. What do the concepts of honesty and honor mean to you?

---

2. Do you expect more honesty or honor from others in your workplace or in your personal life? Explain your rationale.

---

3. Have you experienced an instance when you felt someone was cheating? Do you believe the person realized they were being dishonest or dishonorable? Explain your rationale.

_____
_____
_____
_____
_____

CHAPTER 9: I
INTEGRITY

Integrity without knowledge is weak and useless, and knowledge without integrity is dangerous and dreadful.

—Samuel Johnson

Integrity is defined in *Merriam-Webster's Dictionary* as a "firm adherence to a code" of "moral or artistic values" and "the quality or state of being complete or undivided." An organization without integrity loses its cohesiveness (i.e., what it is made of). Integrity also is important because it appears to be the backbone of good organizational governance, as well as a code of ethics. In fact, an organization that maintains a solid ethical core keeps good employees. According to expert Roger E. Herman in *Keeping Good People* "workers want to be comfortable with what their employer stands for." As a result, Herman suggests that when good employees "sense a strong divergence between their value positions and those of their employer, the likelihood of their divorcing themselves from the employer is greater."

Herman opines that employers can use numerous ethical strategies to retain the best and brightest workers. For example, promoting integrity is one ethical strategy for keeping good people. Herman proposes that an organization can foster a culture based on integrity in several ways, including:

- Stating and restating the desire for honesty and honor in the behavior of all members of the organization.
- Emphasizing the high value the organization places on righteousness.
- Refusing to compromise on organizational and personal values.
- Preparing and abiding by an organizational code of ethics.
- Communicating the organization's expectations that everyone follow the same ethics code with termination being a probable consequence for violating the trust.[32]

An organization that operates with integrity and includes people who use integrity in daily decisions will succeed in the long term. However, the road to maintaining integrity can be difficult to navigate during bad, difficult, or challenging times. For instance, in *The Conduct of Life*, Ralph Waldo Emerson expresses that in "failing circumstances no man can be relied on to keep his integrity."[33] Nonetheless, the true ethical core of a person can be determined during bad, difficult, or challenging times.

One person who demonstrated integrity during an inconvenient occasion was golf legend Bobby Jones. Jones lost the 1925 United States Open golf championship when he penalized himself for accidentally moving his ball in the woods although no one witnessed the transgression.[34] Jones, who believed in golf's emphasis on integrity and honor, was astounded when the self-imposed penalty attracted wide-ranging awe and respect. In response, Jones was reported to have commented, "You might as well have praised a man for not robbing a bank."[35] Jones's approach to personal and professional integrity should be the standard. Jones's ethical framework is echoed by Robert J. Rafalko, assistant professor of philosophy at the University of New Haven: "It is human nature to try to bend the rules and search for loopholes. But when it comes to the question of why business people should obey the law, they usually get one answer: obey or go to jail. This is a powerful message, but there are better answers, like considerations of justice and the need for character, integrity, and honor in our daily lives."[36]

Questions for Reflection or Further Study

1. What person in your life has the most integrity? What person in your life has the least integrity? Which person in your opinion is the most successful? Did integrity impact the level of success for each person?

---

2. What aspects of your organizational culture embrace integrity? What aspects of your organizational culture reject integrity? Do you agree with your organization's approach? Explain your rationale.

_____

_____

_____

_____

3. What would you have done if you were faced with the same circumstances as golf legend Bobby Jones? Does the fact that Jones accidentally moved the golf ball have any impact on his ethical obligations? Explain your rationale.

_____

_____

_____

_____

CHAPTER 10: J
JUSTIFICATION

Quite simply, it is human nature to justify improper behavior. No matter what the behavior is, we try to justify it.

—Robert L. Jolles

Ethics involves asking ourselves questions. These questions probe into our moral insights. A question that most people face at least once in their careers revolves around an age-old query: does the end justify the means? In some instances, especially those that involve strictly moral issues, I believe the end does justify the means. For example, our government decided the end of maintaining order and safe neighborhoods justifies the means of incarcerating men and women as punishment for violating society's laws. In other instances, it may seem that the end does not justify the means. Indeed, most people in our society would not approve of a person's cheating on a job placement examination as a means of obtaining a position.

However, some people struggle with deciding if it is ever okay to perform an immoral act for the benefit of the "greater good."[37] Consider a couple attempting to adopt an infant from an impoverished third world country. The couple hires a lawyer in the country and fulfills the necessary legal requirements. The final step in the adoption is approval by a judge. The couple's adoption case is one of hundreds on the court's docket. The couple's lawyer estimates the adoption case will not be heard by the judge for years based on the country's first-in/first-out system. The lawyer hints that a facilitation payment (which is provided to initiate or "speed-up" a legal process or the provision of services) could get the case moved up the docket. Would the end justify the means if the couple takes the lawyer's advice?

Some people who possess no moral core would commit an immoral act in every instance. Author Robert L. Jolles, in *The Way of the Road Warrior: Lessons in Business and Life from the Road Most Traveled*, notes that a "thief is a thief. A thief will frequently be better at justifying unethical behavior than you are at upholding your ethical attempts to stop it."[38]

In fact, recent sports, business, and political events have illustrated that numerous persons justify improper actions or pursue immoral behavior in order to meet a business objective or achieve personal success. After reports surfaced that National Football League Miami Dolphins running back Ricky Williams tested positive for marijuana in May 2007, David Cornwell, Williams's attorney during the player's substance-abuse hearings with the league, did not acknowledge his client's ethical lapse. Instead, Cronwell justified Williams's apparent relapse on the failure of the NFL "to treat effectively players who are subject to the NFL drug program."[39] Based on an entry written by Carmine Coyote on the Slow Leadership Web site, Williams, as well as others who find themselves justifying their actions, should understand that

- Justification often lies at the heart of unethical behavior.
- Justification relies on devising ways to re-interpret the rules to one's advantage.

Thus, according to Coyote, persons can learn to identify unethical behavior involving justification by reviewing stories and the "flawed thinking that brought smart people down to the level of common criminals."[40]

University of San Francisco director of athletics Debra Gore-Mann acknowledges "people can be tempted to compromise ethics" by "rationaliz[ing]" their actions as it pertains to the organization rather than believe they are "unethical" people.[41] Thus, a visionary organization communicates that justification is not a valid excuse for pursuing behavior inconsistent with its code of ethics.

Questions for Reflection or Further Study

1. When do the ends not justify the means? When do the ends justify the means?

_____

_____

_____

_____

_____

2. What rationale(s) have you or your colleagues used to justify a significant business decision that occurred in the past twelve months? Did the business decision violate the ethical standards of your organization and/or yourself? If yes, how did you feel about using an excuse to violate such standards?

_____

_____

_____

_____

_____

3. What are ways that an organization or person can use to communicate that unethical rationale cannot be used to justify a course of action?

_____

_____

_____

_____

_____

CHAPTER 11: K
KEEPING A PROMISE

We must not promise what we ought not, lest we be called on to perform what we cannot.

—Abraham Lincoln

A promise made is a debt unpaid.

—Robert W. Service

We are taught at an early age that good people always tell the truth and keep promises. We also are cautioned against lying and not fulfilling promises. However, a person can find it difficult to abide by such teachings when failure (e.g., personal or professional) or discomfort (e.g., financial stress) loom on the horizon. In turn, some persons compromise their values and turn their backs on being truthful and honest. The end result is the loss of a person's integrity. A promise made by an organization or person, in and of itself, actually does not show others what the organization or person really stands for. Instead, the integrity of an organization or person is measured by whether the organization or person keeps the promise. Thus, it is an organization or person's fulfillment of a promise, rather than taking the easy way out, that demonstrates its or his/her ethical values.

For example, head football coach Nick Saban of the National Football League Miami Dolphins earned the ire of South Florida professional football fans in early 2007 when he was asked by the media on several occasions to respond to the rumor that he would leave the franchise and assume the head coach position at the University of Alabama. Saban's response: "I'm not going to be the Alabama coach." Saban became the Alabama coach a few weeks later.[42] Although Saban may justify his actions on a variety of reasons (e.g., ongoing negotiations with the university), the coach's lack of honesty and failure to keep a promise left a bitter taste for Dolphin supporters.

In my work as an attorney, private investigator, and consultant, one of the only things a professional can carry from project to project is his or her word. It is essential in dealing with clients, adversaries, witnesses, and other professionals that I maintain my integrity. Otherwise, people will not trust me. If trust in me dissipates for whatever reason, my value to clients, who rely on me to resolve issues effectively and efficiently, decreases. Unfortunately, not all people share the belief that maintaining promises is essential in professional and personal relationships. However, we cannot be deterred by other people's inability or unwillingness to keep a promise. If you make a promise, keep it.

Questions for Reflection or Further Study

1. Have you ever not kept a promise? If yes, what was your rationale? Do you believe your failure to keep the promise was ethical or justified?

_____

_____

_____

_____

_____

2. Are there instances when it is okay not to keep a promise? Explain your rationale.

_____

_____

_____

_____

_____

3. What should an organization or person do when the organization or person determines a promise cannot be kept?

_____

_____

_____

_____

_____

CHAPTER 12: L
LOYALTY

If you pick up a starving dog and make him prosperous, he will not bite you. This is the principle difference between a dog and a man.

—Mark Twain

New friends are silver, but old friends are gold.

—Unknown Author

Loyalty is defined by the *Merriam-Webster's Dictionary* as "the state or quality of being loyal" and loyal as "faithful to a private person to whom fidelity is due" or "faithful to a cause, ideal, custom, institution, or product." Josiah Royce in *The Philosophy of Loyalty* espouses that loyalty is demonstrated when a person makes a morally significant commitment to a cause that he or she deems to be meaningful. Royce believes a person's moral life could be understood in terms of his or her loyalties. He explains that *true loyalty* exists if the moral value of a person's actions satisfies the aim of the cause he or she deemed to be meaningful. He also points out that the greatest moral victories involve a person's loyalty to ideals that advance the creation of causes to which others can express loyalty. In particular, Royce opines "a cause is good, not only for me, but for mankind, in so far as it is essentially a *loyalty to loyalty*, that is, an aid and a furtherance of loyalty in my fellows." In contrast, he dismisses *predatory loyalty*, which is loyalty to immoral causes (as well as sponsors of such causes) and involves "an evil cause in so far as, despite the loyalty that it arouses in me, it is destructive of loyalty in the world of my fellows." In essence, Royce dismisses loyalty attached to a specific group and demonstrated in the subversion or elimination of the context for other persons' loyalties.[43]

The theory of true loyalty is applicable in business and professional relationships. Indeed, Lizabeth England, author of *Language and Civil Society*, notes a "leader must decide between loyalty to the company and truthfulness in business relationships."[44] For example, true loyalty can be

29

found in Toyota Motor Corporation, which has incorporated the concept of *kaizen* (continuous improvement) into company culture. Under *kaizen*, Toyota employees constantly reexamine how the company produces and delivers products and services. Jeff Sutherland, chief technology officer for Scrum Worldwide, explains:

> Toyota employees do not come to work today assuming nothing is broken. They feel that it is a crisis if they do not improve today by changing what they are doing so they do it better. There is no staying in the same place. Either you deteriorate or you move forward. Honesty, transparency, and trust are needed to surface and openly discuss impediments to progress.[45]

As a result, a Toyota employee is expected to be loyal to the ideals of always striving to make the company better and supporting the expression of others.

Examples of predatory loyalty unfortunately are numerous throughout history and in our society. The Ku Klux Klan and the Nazi Party are extreme examples of organizations or causes built on predatory loyalty. Predatory loyalty also exists whenever a business leader promotes officers, managers, and employees who agree with him or her without question and limits the professional progress of those who voice a differing opinion.

Success in business or other professional relationships is dependent on building and maintaining the loyalty of numerous people and groups, from employees to clients and customers. It is our duty to practice true loyalty in daily activities and to eliminate predatory loyalty from the values of an organization.

Questions for Reflection or Further Study

1. What does loyalty mean to you professionally? What does loyalty mean to you personally? Is there a difference in your expectations between your professional and personal lives?

_____

_____

_____

_____

_____

2. Who is the most loyal person in your life (professionally or personally)? How has the person demonstrated their loyalty? Are you as loyal to that person? Why or why not?

_____

_____

_____

_____

3. Do you feel your organization is loyal to you? Why or why not? How does this affect (if at all) your performance?

_____

_____

_____

_____

4. Do you feel that you are loyal to your organization? Why or why not? How does this affect (if at all) your performance?

_____

_____

_____

_____

_____

CHAPTER 13: M
MORALS

That which is beautiful is moral. That is all, nothing more.

—Gustave Flaubert

The foundation of morality is to have done, once and for all, with lying.

—Thomas Henry Huxley

An organization's moral standards can illustrate its ethical approach. Similarly, a person's morals are important to understand his or her ethical behavior. The organization Character Unlimited defines *morals* as "ethical principles" that are "founded on fundamental principles of right conduct rather than legalities."[46] Lander University philosophy professor Dr. Lee C. Archie opines that morals are "a study of human behavior as a consequence of beliefs about what is right or wrong, or good or bad, insofar as that behavior is useful or effective." Archie also adds "morals are the study of what is thought to be right and what is generally done by a group, society, or a culture."[47]

Moral standards may differ between organizations or people. An organization or person's moral standards demonstrates what its members or he or she believes are the group or person's ideas of truth (even if the organization or person's ideal of truth is not consistently practiced). Difficulties arise when two organizations or persons' moral standards are inconsistent. This phenomenon occurs in many aspects of our personal lives (e.g., marriages or other personal relationships) and professional careers (e.g., business deals between organizations from different countries or cultures). However, we can avoid the ethical complexities created by the clash of different moral standards by:

- Identifying the common denominator of right and wrong (no matter how broad or general, a denominator can facilitate further consensus).
- Exploring our duties and responsibilities in the situation.

- Understanding the expectations of the other party in the situation.
- Treating the other party how we would like to be treated in the same circumstance.

The morality of an organization has an impact on the bottom line. A 1997 study released by the Ethics Officer Association, a national organization dedicated to promoting ethical business practices, and the American Society of Chartered Life Underwriters and Chartered Financial Consultants, showed that 16 percent of respondents cut corners on quality control, 14 percent covered up incidents and 11 percent abused or lied about sick days. According to education consultant Dr. B. David Brooks, the unethical behaviors reported in the study have an "impact on profitability, customer relations and internal morale," which are "bottom line" issues.[48] In fact, the standards of right and wrong established by a business organization account for its long-term financially viability. British lord and business leader Brian Griffiths in *Capitalism, Morality and Markets* argues that a "corporation with an effective moral standard will not only have lower transaction costs but will develop over time a strong culture based on trust, so that the adoption of a moral standard will become a source of competitive advantage."[49]

Most importantly, a person should not feel restrained by his or her organization's moral standards. A person may believe that the organizational morals are substantially lower than his or her own personal standards. Unfortunately, many of us take the easy road and resist the urge to do more by relying on what our organization says is moral. For example, Enron Corporation's directors, officers, managers, and employees failed to demand higher ethical standards than those exercised by Kenneth L. Lay and other top executives. Instead, Enron's officers, managers, and employees (and others who are in a similar dilemma) should have heeded the advice of Isaac Asimov, the famous Russian-born American author and biochemist: "Never let your sense of morals get in the way of doing what's right."[50]

Questions for Reflection or Further Study

1. What people, circumstances, or events formed your morals? Explain your rationale.

_____

_____

_____

_____

_____

2. What influences the moral standards of your current organization? How does this affect your work environment?

_____

_____

_____

_____

3. Think about two organizations you belong or belonged to that have had different moral standards. Which organization was more successful (as success is defined by the organization)? Do you think the organizations' moral standards influenced their success? Explain your rationale.

_____

_____

_____

_____

_____

CHAPTER 14: N
NATURE

Nature is an endless combination and repetition of a very few laws.

—Ralph Waldo Emerson

In nature there are neither rewards nor punishments—there are consequences ...

—Robert G. Ingersoll

Nature is no teacher of morality; she herself needs lessons.

—Anonymous

"Human nature, whether it is fixed by genetic endowment or malleable under the influence of social forces, is one of the most hotly debated questions in recent social thought," according to the introduction in an Autumn 1990 issue of *Social Philosophy & Policy*.[51] Human nature is one source for ethical standards. Human nature also is a contributor to the creation, operation, maintenance, and destruction of organizations. In particular, organizations are created (and later grow) as a direct result of people's desire and ability to cooperate with other persons internally and externally. Organizations rely on people being productive (as defined by the organization). The ethics of an organization should reflect the standards, principles, and values that permit persons within the organization to fulfill their roles. Moreover, the ethical framework of an organization should address the manner in which persons who produce and cooperate resolve the issues, tribulations, and evils caused by those who do not abide by the same standards.

Northeastern Illinois University, Chicago, justice studies professor T. Y. Okosun, in a university Web site article, analyzes the relationship of human nature and ethics in business organizations:

> Business on the other hand is not inherently ethical, but is an associated ele-
> ment of the human nature—which I insist is neither good nor bad, ethical

35

or unethical, and so on. Since human nature is what it is as such—and business is one of its many elements, it is quite possible to say that business is not inherently ethical but implicated and recognizable in the domain of human nature.[52]

The ethical success of an organization (whether the organization is created for business, charity, or other purposes) is related to the extent that people curb the selfish aspects of human nature. However, some parts of our society excuse the transgressions of other persons as long as they are prosperous or able to make the organization successful.

For example, the National Football League Atlanta Falcons came under scrutiny for failing to confront quarterback Michael Vick concerning a "series of recent off-the-field incidents, most recently an ongoing investigation of illegal dog fighting at a property he owns in Virginia."[53] Vick is one of the most physically gifted players in professional football. Vick generated millions of dollars for himself, the Falcons, and the NFL as a result of his unique style of play. However, according to a May 10, 2007, *Sports Illustrated* Web site article, Vick's "troubling pattern of recent behavior reflects a penchant for questionable judgment, an unwillingness to distance himself from the wrong crowd, and a long-standing belief that the rules don't apply to him."[54] Although it was reported on May 11, 2007, that the Falcons owner had a "stern" talk with Vick after the illegal dog fighting investigation surfaced[55], the franchise had been accused in the past of excusing Vick's behavior. In fact, *Sports Illustrated* reported "it's obvious the Falcons organization bears some responsibility for his troubling pattern of behavior. Team owner Arthur Blank has been too quick to either coddle Vick or excuse his actions, even after Vick creates headlines that embarrass the organization."[56] Vick's 2009 return to the NFL will show human nature in action—I hope the star athlete used his incarceration for dog fighting to change his life and behavior.

The inclination to excuse ethical transgressions results in an organization operating on a lower set of ethical standards. Leaders and managers, according to Sandy Barbour, the director of athletics at the University of California, Berkeley, are responsible for upholding ethical standards.[57] I concur with Barbour. In fact, I believe that organizations that adhere to a high ethical standard have discovered ways to curb the selfish aspect of human nature and encourage people to make ethical decisions.

Questions for Reflection or Further Study

1. Name an organization that was successful despite some or all of its members displaying unethical behavior. What was the rationale for the success?

_____

_____

_____

_____

2. What organization do you know of has been the most successful at curbing the selfish aspects of human nature? What methods did the organization use to achieve this result? Can such methods be successfully applied in other organizations?

_____

_____

_____

_____

_____

CHAPTER 15: O
OBSTACLES

Man is most uniquely human when he turns obstacles into opportunities.

—Eric Hoffer

The gem cannot be polished without friction.

—Chinese proverb

An ethical organization or person is one who adheres to ethical standards and maintains the pursuit of profits and success even in the face of obstacles. Anyone can operate a profitable business or achieve personal success in good times, but it is during difficult times that the measure of an organization or person is illustrated. Obstacles in an organization or person's path highlight its or his/her integrity. Why? It is easier to circumvent societal rules, ignore organizational standards, and shun personal values when stress abounds, deadlines loom, laws tighten, and competition increases. Nevertheless, I have learned through my professional career and personal life that it is even more important to take the high road and aspire to a strict ethical standard in the face of temptation and hurdles.

Unfortunately, I have observed or dealt with numerous persons who take the easy way out to solve a problem, pursue a business goal, or represent a client. For example, in a few of my sports investigation cases, private regulatory agency investigators and legal counsel for involved parties have resorted to mischaracterizing facts and omitting the existence of oral agreements to avoid admitting a mistake and facing the resulting consequences.

It is inevitable that we will come out on the painful side of the equation on a few occasions when an organization, a competitor, or other person does not adhere to ethical standards when faced with hurdles and difficulties. However, it is important for persons desiring to pursue an ethical path to remember to adhere to the highest values and standards. As an unknown author once remarked, "Adversity introduces a man to himself."

Questions for Reflection or Further Study

1. List the three most challenging, difficult, or inconvenient occasions you have faced in your life. What decisions did you make to address each situation? Do you feel each decision was ethical? Explain your rationale.

_____

_____

_____

_____

_____

2. List three examples of organizations or persons who confronted challenges or hurdles. How did each organization or person handle the challenge or hurdle? Did the way the organization or person chose to handle the challenge or hurdle adhere to its/his/her stated ethical standard or code?

_____

_____

_____

_____

_____

CHAPTER 16: P
PREVENTIVE MAINTENANCE

Our primary objective is to prevent ethics violations before they occur.

—New York State Ethics Commission Web site Welcome
Statement

Leaders and managers who are intent on supporting ethical behavior should learn to identify, on a proactive basis, potential ethics problems in their organizations. A proactive approach allows management to address ethics problems before they become substantial "financial, legal, and public relations nightmares" according to author Christopher Bauer in a *The CEO Refresher* article. This proactive approach, also referred to as *preventive maintenance*, is one method to address ethical issues. According to Bauer, most organizational leaders and ethics training programs "overlook the fact that the vast majority of ethics violations have their roots in personal matters that have little or nothing to do with knowledge of the ethics code." He explains ethical "violations typically have to do with personal wishes and values 'rubbing' with the mandates of ethical or legal behavior and that 'rub' goes either unseen or unaddressed until it is too late."

However, organizations can develop initiatives to address this reality. For instance, Bauer notes organizations can create a culture "in which ethically-attuned decision making is modeled and rewarded." Also, organizations can develop means to assist employees "take personal responsibility for 'walking the talk' of ethics." This requires an organization to provide its employees "with the climate, concepts and tools" to successfully maintain these initiatives. An ethically-sensitive climate allows organizational culture to change "from supporting the existing 'reactive' response to ethical challenges to a focus on the active, effective prevention of problems." In addition, in this new climate, the role of compliance is refocused from a "back-up" system to "the front line effort to deal with issues of ethics."[58] Sandy Barbour, the director of athletics at the University of California, Berkeley, stresses that leaders and managers are responsible for upholding ethical standards. Barbour believes "ethics has to be recognized and incentivized" by leaders and managers. For example, the University of California athletics department recognizes people who demonstrate ethical behavior with annual awards and honors. According to Barbour, the athletics department's commitment to recognize ethical employees shows "what we stand for and champion."[59]

As a result, leaders and managers should not tolerate an attitude or culture that ignores ethical transgressions. Organizations that permit employees to commit an insignificant ethical violation without suffering any meaningful consequence create a progressive environment that breeds significant unethical practices. For example, a mid-1990s illicit accounting scheme operated by Joseph Jett, a bond trader for then General Electric subsidiary Kidder, Peabody and Company, illustrates the importance of preventive maintenance. According to an investigation by the Securities and Exchange Commission (SEC), Kidder's "bond department revenues under Jett's watch climbed from six to twenty-seven percent in a one-year period," which "defied all reasonable explanations." Jett received a $9 million bonus. However, the SEC determined "Jett's supervisor did not ask the hard, ethical questions, and some employees were even dismissed for raising concerns about Jett's outsized performance." The scandal and lawsuits arising out of Jett's unethical behavior forced General Electric to sell Kidder at a $600 million loss in 1994. Professor Marianne M. Jennings and journalist Jon Entine in a 1998 *Hamline Journal of Public Law & Policy* article on the Jett-Kidder case noted "a firm's refusal or reluctance to examine potential illegal activity or turn a blind-eye to an obvious disparity possesses a tarnished soul."[60]

Questions for Reflection or Further Study

1. Does your organization have a culture that rewards or encourages decision making that is consistent with a stated ethical standards or code? Describe the culture. Also, explain if the culture enhances the organization's core business.

_____

_____

_____

_____

_____

2. Does your organization have a program or provide resources to assist employees with taking personal responsibility for making ethical decisions? Does the program or resources work effectively? Explain your rationale.

_____

_____

_____

_____

3. What are your goals and desires (professionally and personally)? List the three most important activities, decisions, issues, or goals that you believe need to be addressed within the next twelve months. Do your goals, desires, or pending decisions have an impact on your ethical outlook? Explain your rationale.

_____

_____

_____

_____

4. Does your organization possess a system to identify potential ethical issues? Does your organization tolerate minor ethical violations? Explain if the way your organization addresses potential or current ethical issues creates an environment that encourages unethical practices. What could be done to encourage ethical behavior?

_____

_____

_____

_____

CHAPTER 17: Q
QUARREL

We are never so much disposed to quarrel with others as when we are dissatisfied with ourselves.

—William Hazlitt

Quarrels would not last long if the fault were on one side only.

—La Rochefoucauld

There is no such test of a man's superiority of character as in the well-conducting of an unavoidable quarrel; and to be engaged in no quarrels but those that are unavoidable.

—Henry Taylor

In a *Harvard Business Review* article, Albert Carr relates "the familiar story of the shopkeeper who finds an extra twenty-dollar bill in the cash register, debates with himself the ethical problem—should he tell his partner?—and finally decides to share the money because the gesture will give him an edge over the s.o.b. the next time they quarrel." Carr uses the story to claim an "illusion" exists "that business can afford to be guided by ethics as conceived in private life." Carr notes that "talk about ethics by businessmen is often a thin decorative coating over the hard realities of the game." In fact, he argues "that in the long run a company can make more money if it does not antagonize competitors, suppliers, employees, and customers by squeezing them too hard." Carr opines this "has nothing to do with ethics."[61]

I agree with Carr that some organizations "talk a good game" to avoid disputes, problems with employees, customers, clients, competitors, and suppliers. We are bombarded with chief executives and other leaders who trump their organization's high ethical standards and codes. Events show that for several of these organizations the talk about high ethical standards is just that—talk. These organizations believe that ethics is part of a public relations or marketing strategy.

However, I believe that it is possible for an organization, including businesses, to adhere to a high set of ethical standards. An organization can have a fancy code of ethics, but it is in vain if the people who belong to the group do not follow their own person ethical standards that mimic or exceed those of the organization.

For example, the Salt Lake City Winter Olympic corruption scandal tarnished the previously sterling ethical reputation of the international Olympic movement.[62] According to news reports, excessive gifts and other benefits were provided to decision makers in an effort to influence the International Olympic Committee's selection of Salt Lake City, Utah, to host the 2002 Winter Olympics. The scandal showed some members of the international organization had strayed from the IOC's ethical standards.[63] The investigation of the bribery allegations resulted in quarreling, conflict, and mistrust among IOC members, athletic organizations, governments, and the public. The IOC addressed the investigation's findings by expelling members and revamping the selection process for awarding future Olympic games to host cities.[64] The controversy reminded the IOC that an organization that is guided by an ethical code and attracts people who aspire to their own ethical standard will refrain from engaging in unnecessary quarrels, disputes, fights, or altercations with employees, customers, clients, competitors, and suppliers.

Questions for Reflection or Further Study

1. How does your organization communicate its ethical standards or code? Do you believe that your organization's communications are genuine or one aspect of a marketing/public relations campaign?

2. List three organizations or professionals who boasted about ethical standards in the past twelve months. How did the message come across to you?

3. Does an employee's personal ethical standards affect his or her organizational ethical behavior? Explain your rationale.

_____

_____

_____

_____

4. The head of a sales department for a small, but growing, corporation is in the final stages of completing a deal with a major client for a large sale of parts. The sales head has worked on the deal for over two years. The deal would enhance the corporation's clout in the industry, as well as provide a steady cash flow for three years. In the final meeting before the deal is consummated, the client requests the head of sales to prepare the sale agreements in such a manner so that the client can avoid triggering various tax laws in the client's home state. If you were the sales head, what would you do? Explain your rationale.

_____

_____

_____

_____

_____

CHAPTER 18: R
DEFINING WHAT IS RIGHT
AND WRONG

It is never too late to do right.

—Ralph Waldo Emerson

There are many things which in and of themselves seem morally right, but which under certain circumstances prove to be not morally right.

—Marcus Tullius Cicero

The time is always ripe to do right.

—Reverend Dr. Martin Luther King, Jr.

Always do right. This will gratify some people and astonish the rest.

—Mark Twain

How does our understanding of right and wrong influence our ethical behavior? Some people believe that ethical decisions of right and wrong depend on the situation or circumstances. For instance, I was taught at an early age that copying answers from a fellow student's exam was cheating and, thus, wrong behavior. However, it is common to be offered a pirated copy of a motion picture by unscrupulous sellers—even when the movie being offered recently premiered. In fact, many people do not find it wrong to copy a person's musical work or a studio's motion picture. The existence of technology may be one reason for this phenomenon. In particular, some people believe that technology provides a device that covers or shades a person's actions from the outside world. With the advent of compact disc burning devices and music-sharing Web sites, it is easier and faster to copy an artist's musical work online than it is to travel to a music store and shoplift an album. Technology makes the act of stealing antiseptic.

Laws and regulations also cloud many people on what is right and wrong. For example, some organizations and persons rely on what has been passed by our country's federal and state legislatures as defining what is right and wrong. However, simply being permitted by the federal, state, or local government does not make that action ethically right. For instance, the legality of slavery and the inability of women and minorities to vote are examples of previous American laws that could not be substantiated under ethical standards.

What is right, and what is wrong? An answer can be developed by sampling insights into moralistic behavior. According to coauthors Manuel Velasquez, Claire Andre, Thomas Shanks, and Michael J. Meye in an *Issues in Ethics* article, ethical relativism can provide guidance on the question of right and wrong. The authors describe ethical relativism as "the theory that holds that morality is relative to the norms of one's culture." Further, they argue "an action is right or wrong depend[ing] on the moral norms of the society in which it is practiced." Under this notion, an "action may be morally right in one society but be morally wrong in another." The authors also explain that people who espouse ethical relativism believe "there are no universal moral standards," but "the only moral standards against which a society's practices can be judged are its own."[65] I do not concur with their conclusion, but offer it to illustrate the differing interpretation of ethical concepts. Instead, I believe that all societies and cultures share a common dominator of right and wrong. Due to the global economy, the various nations on this planet cannot effectively and efficiently operate under varying ethical standards.

Another way to judge what is right and wrong is to refer to the outcome or consequence of the particular action. I concur with this approach to defining what is right and wrong. In *All About Hinduism*, author Sri Swami Sivananda concludes behavior is "correct" if it "is worthy of achievement."[66] Similarly, William Penn, the founder the Commonwealth of Pennsylvania, once remarked "What is wrong is wrong, even if everyone is doing it. Right is still right, even if no one else is doing it."[67] For example, a decision may be ethically right if it results in generating the most good for the greatest amount of organizations, interests, or people. Sandy Barbour, the director of athletics at the University of California, Berkeley, explains that the ethical framework that guides her organization is based on one premise: "Do the right thing." She observes, "Ethics and integrity are frequently commingled and confused." Consequently, Barbour notes, "For us setting the framework for what constitutes doing the right thing" is crucial in maintaining an ethical organization. For example, Barbour's leadership style requires the institution's athletics administrators, staff, and student-athletes to "think about their actions and behavior and how the [actions and behavior] affect" others.[68] Similarly, the leadership model for Debra Gore-Mann, the director of athletics at the University of San Francisco, centers on "doing the right thing," which involves a "commitment to integrity and an expectation for excellence." Ms. Gore-Mann explains all "conversations" in her decision-making process "always" require answers to two fundamental questions: "What is best for student-athletes? Does it treat people with respect and dignity?"[69] Thus, an organization or person can best define what is right and wrong by determining the ultimate impact of a decision or activity on society or other parties.

Questions for Reflection or Further Study

1. What is your definition of right and wrong? Do your actions follow your definition in all aspects of your professional and personal lives? Explain your rationale.

_____

_____

_____

_____

2. What is your organization's definition of right and wrong? Do your organization's actions follow its definition in the pursuit of its operational goals? Explain your rationale.

_____

_____

_____

_____

3. How can people determine if a particular decision or action is right or wrong?

_____

_____

_____

_____

4. Have you ever witnessed or heard about an employee who: a) shops online for personal items using the company computer during work hours; b) uses organizational supplies (e.g., pens, paper, copy machine) for personal use; c) provides clients or customers with a falsehood or misrepresentation to defuse

a dispute? Is the employee right or wrong? Determine the ethical nature of each hypothetical situation.

_____

_____

_____

_____

_____

CHAPTER 19: S
SELLING YOUR REPUTATION

You can't build a reputation on what you are going to do.

—Henry Ford

Worldly wisdom teaches that it is better for reputation to fail conventionally than to succeed unconventionally.

—John Maynard Keynes

Many consult their reputation; but few their conscience.

—Publius Syrus

In my line of work, as in most other occupations, trades, and professions, my business is dependant on my reputation. In particular, the manner in which an organization or person treats someone or something else is the basis for the organization's or person's reputation. Most importantly, the ability of an organization or person to maintain the trust of clients, customers, co-workers, employees, vendors, shareholders, and stakeholders is the key for upholding an ethical reputation. The importance of protecting our reputation is one reason most organizations and persons engage in various measures to ensure policies and procedures are legal and full of integrity and adhere to a defined standard of ethical behavior. Employees, clients, customers, vendors, and others are attracted to organizations and persons who adhere to a high standard of ethics and integrity.

In fact, research conducted by Stanford University professor David B. Montgomery and University of California, Santa Barbara, professor Catherine A. Ramus is relevant to this issue. Their March 2003 preliminary study with 279 MBAs from two European and three North American business schools revealed "reputation-related attributes of caring about employees, environmental sustain-ability, community/stakeholder relations, and ethical products and services are important in job choice decisions." Further, the researchers determined "that more than ninety percent of the MBAs in the sample were willing to forgo financial benefits in order to work for an organization with a better reputation for corporate social responsibility and ethics."[70]

Sadly, too many organizations and persons believe that an ethical reputation is important to manage only when it is beneficial to a marketing or public relations campaign. For instance, in an April 29, 2004, presentation at the University of Texas, Austin, McCombs School of Business, Ron Alsop, a senior editor with *The Wall Street Journal* and author of *The 18 Immutable Laws of Corporate Reputation*, noted, "Most companies only focus on their reputations in times of trouble. Successful players tend their reputations all the time."[71] For example, in January 2003, Philip Morris changed its name to Altria Group to clarify "the corporate structure—the relationship of the parent to its operating companies," which include such "globally recognized brands as Marlboro, Kraft, Parliament, Oreo, Ritz, Virginia Slims and Oscar Mayer."[72] Philip Morris's marketing strategy was in response to the public's heightened focus on the harmful effects of tobacco products on consumers.[73]

Organizations and professionals can build or maintain a reputation for ethical behavior by adhering to a stringent code of ethics. This means developing a code, not just for show or public consumption, and injecting the stated ethical standards in every decision or action—including making hiring decisions, developing a new product line, or advertising the latest service offering.

Questions for Reflection or Further Study

1. How would you describe your professional and personal reputation? Do you believe your professional or personal reputations are different? Explain your rationale.

_____

_____

_____

_____

2. Describe your organization's reputation among clients and customers, among peers in your organization's industry, and among the general public. Explain any differences. Also, explain what impact your organization's reputation has on the organization's stated business goals.

_____

_____

_____

_____

3. What methods are used by your organization to protect its reputation? Do any of the methods address ethical behavior? Why or why not?

_____

_____

_____

_____

_____

CHAPTER 20: T
TRUST

It is better to trust virtue than fortune.

—Publius Syrus

How many times do you get to lie before you are a liar?

—Michael Josephson

Trustworthiness is an asset an organization or person should possess. In fact, according to author Dr. Charles E. Watson in *What Smart People Do When Dumb Things Happen at Work,* great leaders handle "everyday situations in ways that earn them the full confidence of others" by "living by their commitments, not calculations" and "going out of their way to live by their word." Watson recounts advice proffered by then DuPont chairman and chief executive officer Richard E. Heckert to business students. Heckert's advice was simple, yet profound: "Do what you say you are going to do; keep your promises, especially if it's inconvenient for you. Go out of your way to act responsibly.... They will come to realize you are dependable. People will know you can be trusted to keep your word."[74] Heckert's wisdom underscores the fact that keeping promises builds trust.

In turn, trust is a component of integrity. Regardless of political affiliation, then New York City mayor Rudy Giuliani's leadership style after the 9/11 attacks endeared him to Americans who craved leaders that they felt had integrity and that they could trust. The recognition of trust as an element of ethical behavior can propel an organization or a person to the higher echelon of companies and professionals. Business is full of risk and uncertainty. The existence of trust permits a client, customer, vendor, shareholder, or employee to bridge the gap of risk and uncertainty and rely on the judgment, actions, or decision-making of an organization or person.

For example, low-cost air carrier Southwest has generated a loyal customer base by providing a consistent product that people trust. Southwest's business model and practices built a "bank" of trust—into which the airline consistently made "deposits" of customer-focused, consistent, and dependable service—over decades. The airline draws on its trust bank when service mistakes occur.[75] The Southwest example illustrates that being trustworthy is necessary to conduct business and crucial to be successful in the long-term.

Questions for Reflection or Further Study

1. What person do you trust the most? How was the trust developed? Do you model your behavior, actions, or decisions along the same lines?

2. Do you trust the leaders of your organization? Why or why not?

3. Do you believe that the clients, customers, or stakeholders of your organization trust it? Why or why not? Does the level of trust each have in your organization affect its business goals?

CHAPTER 21: U
UNSELFISHNESS

The essence of man, his uniqueness, is in his power to surpass the self, to rise above his needs and selfish motives.

—Abraham Joshua Heschel

You have not lived a perfect day, even though you have earned your money, unless you have done something for someone who cannot repay you.

—Ruth Smeltzer

You must be fit to give before you can be fit to receive.

—James Stephens

Compassion is the basis of morality.

—Arthur Schopenhauer

The ability to ignore our inherent nature to be selfish, as well as to base our actions on a concern for other persons, is an aspect of ethical behavior. Another word for unselfishness is *altruism.* University of San Diego philosophy professor Lawrence M. Hinman in *Ethics: A Pluralistic Approach to Ethical Theory* defines altruism as a "selfless concern for other people purely for their own sake."[76] French philosopher Auguste Comte, who developed the term altruism, argues in *Catechisme Positiviste* that people possess a moral obligation to renounce self-centeredness and live for other persons. In fact, Comte lectured that the highest standards of ethical behavior impose a moral obligation on a person to serve other parties rather than him-or herself.[77] Essentially, all codes of ethics contain some element of altruism. The codes demand we promote other persons before our interests. However, altruism does not mean not to care for ourselves or our organizations. The concept guides us to perform good acts without an expectation for a reward or honor.

Altruism is best embodied in the golden rule as articulated by author and speaker John C. Maxwell in *There's No Such Thing as "Business" Ethics: There's Only One Rule for Making Decisions*: "How would I like to be treated in this situation?" Maxwell argues that asking the above question would provide anyone with "an integrity guideline for *any* situation."[78] Some may argue that following the golden rule is not practical in business or other professional endeavors. In fact, it can be argued that the idea of fulfilling the needs of others before an organization's own needs directly contradicts the tenets of capitalism. However, numerous corporations' adoption of environmental (e.g., Starbucks's promotion of "green" issues[79]) and social (e.g., Delta Air Lines's active sponsorship of Habitat for Humanity[80]) causes demonstrates that altruism can work in a capitalist society. Thus, our ethical obligation to have a concern for others in decision-making incorporates the golden rule.

Questions for Reflection or Further Study

1. List three examples of an organization or professional making a decision or engaging in an activity that could be described as unselfish. Did the organization or professional derive any benefit from the unselfish act? Was the unselfish act promoted in any way by the organization or professional? If yes, did the promotion in and of itself lessen the unselfish act?

_____

_____

_____

_____

2. List three occasions when you committed an altruistic act. How did you feel afterwards?

_____

_____

_____

_____

_____

3. Describe how you handled the three most challenging, difficult, or inconvenient instances that faced you or your organization during the past twelve months. Were your decisions in each situation unselfish or altruistic? Explain your rationale.

_____

_____

_____

_____

_____

CHAPTER 22: V
VALUES

Authentic values are those by which a life can be lived, which can form a people that produces great deeds and thoughts.

—Allan Bloom

Without commonly shared and widely entrenched moral values and obligations, neither the law, nor democratic government, nor even the market economy, will function properly.

—Václav Havel

Political debates in recent times have included banter concerning "American values." Persons from earlier generations reminisce about the values of yesteryear. But what are values? Also, what importance do values play into the formation of an ethical standard? The organization Character Unlimited defines *values* as "refer[ing] to all important beliefs," but notes that "not all [values] are ethical, some are neutral or non-ethical." The organization's definition also differentiates between a "stated" value, which is described as "what we say," and an "operational" value, which is characterized as "what we do."[81]

Values also can be described as something that is essential to or prized by a party. Values are what an organization (as well as professionals within the organization) deems to be correct, just, and right. Values can be seen as the moral, ethical, and professional characteristics of the organization, including the characteristics that officers and employees are expected to exemplify. Essentially, values are what an organization represents internally and externally, as well as the foundation for the conduct taken toward parties associated with it.

The discussion of values also is crucial to the contemplation of an organization's vision. In fact, an organization's values and vision must be consistent in order to achieve its stated goals. Thus, the adherence by all stakeholders to a values statement that is consistent with the overall vision of an organization can be an excellent method for implementing various decision-making processes throughout the organization. Further, stated values that are consistent with the vision of an organization ensure that all stakeholders are making decisions, contemplating plans, implementing activities, and pursuing various agenda in the same direction and for the identical purpose. As a result, values enable the organization (and its members) to succeed in its stated business or purpose along the lines of what it deemed to be important.

However, in instances when an organization does not possess a consistent set of values or when stakeholders' actions are not consistent with the organization's stated values, the organization becomes vulnerable. An organization that does not embrace a culture based on a set of values will have the stability of its operations and systems undermined as a result of dysfunction, inefficiency, and ineffectiveness. Bob Bowlsby, director of athletics at Stanford University, advises leaders, managers, and administrators to "hire people who exemplify" the ethical values of the organization. Leaders should "identify, articulate, exemplify, and perpetuate appropriate values in the organization." Mr. Bowlsby notes it is "important for the person to have a vision" and to "put the vision in the daily workings of the organization." This leadership model creates a working environment in which the vision "perpetuates in the overall fabric" of the organization.[82] Similarly, University of San Francisco director of athletics Debra Gore-Mann believes that as an organizational leader, "the buck stops with us." Ms. Gore-Mann adds leaders "have to educate and communicate," as well as "follow-up."[83]

Most important, an organization must be aware of the difference between its stated values and working values. The stated values are the principles that an organization publishes, for a variety of reasons, in a number of devices (e.g., Web site, annual report, employee handbook). Working values are the principles that actually steer the decision making and behavior of the organization. In some organizations, the manner in which an organization operates on a daily basis is inconsistent with its stated values. Most organizations include honesty and integrity in stated core values. However, some organizations have been cited for terminating or demoting employees who report instances of fraud or misconduct. For example, a July 29, 2004, *USA Today* article highlights the story of one "whistleblower," Mark Livingston. Livingston filed a federal lawsuit against pharmaceutical company Wyeth under the federal Sarbanes-Oxley law. The lawsuit alleges that Livingston "lost his job as a quality control manager at Wyeth because he complained repeatedly about manufacturing practices for a vaccine that the Centers for Disease Control and Prevention says is given to about 60%

of infants."[84] Ironically, Wyeth's core values include a pledge to "operate ethically" and "communicate in an honest and authentic manner."[85] These organizations not only operate along inconsistent value frameworks, but the working values of the organizations discourage behavior that will ultimately enhance the stated core business. Further, inconsistent stated and working values sow distrust and doubt in the minds of the organizations' employees. This, in turn, will weaken organizations and create discontent. This can be prevented through the consistency and communication of values in all organizations.

Questions for Reflection or Further Study

1. What are your personal values?

_____

_____

_____

_____

2. What are the values of your organization?

_____

_____

_____

_____

3. Are the values you have and your organization states consistent? If the values are inconsistent, does the inconsistency affect your job performance? Explain your rationale.

_____

_____

_____

_____

4. Is it important or proper for an organization to inquire as to a prospective employee's values before hiring him or her? Explain your rationale.

_____

_____

_____

_____

CHAPTER 23: W
WALKING THE EXTRA MILE

The most important thing in any relationship is not what you get but what you give.

—Eleanor Roosevelt

The best place to find a helping hand is at the end of your own arm.

—Swedish proverb

According to evangelist Keith Sharp in a *Truth Magazine* article, a solider in the ancient Roman army could compel a person from a conquered territory to carry a load one mile. Thus, "walking the first mile" describes a party's obligation to do what is required by duty or other authority. However, an organization or person who possesses a strong ethical core will complete the required distance and walk an extra mile. In this context, "walking an extra mile" translates into providing a positive influence for, or benefit to, others.[86]

Author and speaker John C. Maxwell notes in *There's No Such Thing as "Business" Ethics: There's Only One Rule for Making Decisions* that walking an extra mile is accomplished by making a "positive impact on the lives of others, to add value to people." For example, Maxwell describes a person who walks an extra mile as someone who cares, risks, dreams, expects, and works more than others believe is wise, practicable, necessary, or possible.[87] Refrigeration Research, a family-owned company that manufactures component refrigeration parts, is one organization that expects the organization to walk the extra mile. One provision of Refrigeration Research's company policy explains a "company must be willing to 'Walk the Extra Mile' for the customer. When all usual and expected duties have been performed for the customer but unusual needs arise, the supplier must be willing to 'Walk the Extra Mile' in providing assistance to the customer."[88] In our professional career and personal life, we adhere to a strong ethical framework by going out of our way to provide others with something of value when it is not required or expected.

Questions for Reflection or Further Study

1. List at least one person in your professional or personal life who you believe "walks the extra mile." Describe why the person's actions demonstrate the principle of walking the extra mile.

_____

_____

_____

_____

_____

2. Do you walk the "extra mile?" Explain your rationale.

_____

_____

_____

_____

_____

CHAPTER 24: X
XENOPHOBIA

It's what people know about themselves inside that makes them afraid.

—Ernest Tidyman

Fear not only anticipates misfortunes that never happen, it also precipitates some that would not otherwise have happened.

—Anonymous

A fear of the unknown, or *xenophobia*, can have an impact on our ethical outlook. *Merriam-Webster's Dictionary* defines xenophobia as a "fear and hatred of strangers or foreigners or of anything that is strange or foreign." History is full of instances when a society's fear of ideas, people, organizations, or ideas caused it to respond in ways that required its members to behave, perform, or act in a manner that was inconsistent with their professional and personal ethical standards. For example, due to the fear of slave owners, it was illegal in many American states during the nineteenth century for white persons to teach African slaves or freed blacks to read. However, this law was inconsistent with the personal ethical standards of numerous persons who sacrificed severe punishment to teach reading to slaves and freedmen. In 1853, for instance, Margaret Douglas was indicted by a grand jury and eventually sentenced to prison in Virginia for operating a school for free black children in a back room of her Norfolk house.[89]

It is important for us to recognize when fear or hatred exists. Afterwards, it is crucial for us to use whatever means to ensure these feelings do not result in behavior that is inconsistent with ethical standards. For example, organizations, especially multi-national corporations, can initiate strategies to confront xenophobia. One approach is an organization's implementation of education and training programs "to improve the relationship between people of different races, religions and cultures." Further, organizations should define and observe standards of non-discrimination and fair treatment for all employees.[90]

Questions for Reflection or Further Study

1. List three instances in which a fear or hatred of something was the foundation for a law, rule, or policy that fostered unethical behavior.

_____

_____

_____

_____

2. What can you do to promote ethical behavior in the face of fear or hatred?

_____

_____

_____

_____

3. How can an organization or a person adhere to an ethical standard while protecting against a real or perceived danger or threat?

_____

_____

_____

_____

_____

CHAPTER 25: Y
YIELDING

For he who lives as passion directs will not hear argument that dissuades him, nor understand it if he does; and how can we persuade one in such a state to change his ways? And in general passion seems to yield not to argument but to force.

—Aristotle

First, when a conflict arises between ethics and law, psychologists "make known their commitment to the Ethics Code." Thus, even though an obligation under the Ethics Code may ultimately yield to a legal obligation, psychologists must nonetheless indicate in some fashion that they have a contrary obligation under their profession's code of ethics.

—Dr. Stephen Behnke (writing on the American Psychological Association new ethics code)

A comprehensive code of ethics sets a standard of integrity, values, purpose, and professionalism for an organization. An organization that strictly follows its code of ethics does so even in the midst of difficulty or inconvenience. In other words, an ethical organization does not yield to temptations, emotions, trends, or justifications. Instead, it will make ethical decisions despite internal and external forces that promote questionable behavior.

As explained by Edward B. Nufer, author of an article in *The National Teaching & Learning Forum*, the development of a "code of ethics has nothing to do with being preachy or claiming moral high ground," but addresses "the practical realization" that all persons, including professionals, "face difficult situations, and need to exercise sophisticated judgment." Nufer explains that a "functional ethical framework offers a powerful tool—a compass—in carrying out this work." Most importantly, Nufer notes that a "code of ethics resists yielding to the moment."[91] For example, as reported by *The Wall Street Journal,* young business executives learned the lessons of yielding to internal and external pressures during an ethical business simulation test:

For the young executives at computer-maker InfoMaster Ltd., the company budget was on the line. Terrorism threats were swirling in Jakarta, Indonesia, and the company had to either shut down production there for one quarter and harden security or keep churning out hot-selling products. The executives opted for production over protection. Soon after, a bomb exploded at the plant. "I just killed 350 people," said a dazed David Marye, InfoMaster's 25year-old chief ethics officer. "I made a bad call, and people died. It's going to be hard to sleep tonight." Luckily for Mr. Marye, both InfoMaster and the terrorist attack were fictitious, part of an elaborate game created last year by the University of Texas at Austin's McCombs School of Business.... The real intent was to teach students about handling the delicate balance of business and ethics, and the sometimes high moral price of too much cost cutting.[92]

Accordingly, an organizational code of ethics assists organizations and persons with making the right judgments when the decision-making process is influenced by factors that favor unethical choices.

Questions for Reflection or Further Study

1. List three instances when you or your organization yielded to the moment and sacrificed ethical standards. What were the consequences?

_____

_____

_____

_____

2. What can an organization or person do to protect against yielding in face of pressure or other influences?

_____

_____

_____

_____

CHAPTER 26: Z
ZERO TOLERANCE

We are none of us tolerant in what concerns us deeply and entirely.

—Samuel Taylor Coleridge

If there is but one truth, and you have that truth completely, toleration of differences means an encouragement to error, crime, evil, sin.

—Crane Brinton

A culture of zero tolerance for unethical behavior is a requirement for any organization or person upholding the highest values. Since organizations are comprised of individuals, it is imperative for each of us to incorporate a culture of zero tolerance in our professional careers and personal lives. The number of cases and scandals involving ethical misconduct in recent years dictates that clients, customers, shareholders, stakeholders, and others impose zero tolerance on ethical lapses. However, organizations and persons with a history of commitment to the highest ethical standards will not have problems meeting this expectation. In fact, a company whose business practices meets or exceeds the average ethical framework will have zero tolerance for unethical behavior exhibited by its directors, officers, employees, vendors, and suppliers.

An organizational culture of zero tolerance takes many forms, including:

- Recognizing that ethical standards are applied to everyone and everything consistently and fairly.
- Creating a culture that encourages discussion of ethical issues, questions, and topics.
- Creating a procedure for the reporting of unethical or questionable behavior or practices.
- Conducting comprehensive ethical education and training programs for all directors, officers, managers, employees, suppliers, vendors, and other relevant parties.

- Addressing instances of unethical conduct in a consistent and open manner.
- Declining to make decisions that are legal, but inconsistent with the organization's core values and code of ethics.
- Providing persons within the organization with the necessary support and resources to ensure compliance with ethical standards.

Questions for Reflection or Further Study

1. Explain your organization's methods to promote zero tolerance for unethical behavior. Do the methods work? What would be your recommendation?

_____

_____

_____

_____

2. Explain your methods to promote zero tolerance for unethical behavior in your professional career and personal life. Do the methods work?

_____

_____

_____

_____

3. Is it okay for an organization or person to relax very high ethical standards? Explain the circumstances.

_____

_____

_____

_____

_____

ENDNOTES

1. Claire Andre and Manuel Velasquez, *"What is Ethics?,"* Issues in Ethics 1, no. 1 (Fall 1987): n.p., http://www.scu.edu/ethics/publications/iie/v1n1/ whatis.html (accessed May 7, 2007).

2. Jean Marmoreo and Bob Ramsay, *"About Us,"* JeansMarines, http://www.jeansmarines.com/about_us.asp (accessed May 7, 2007).

3. Unnati Gandhi, *"Marine Corps Marathon threatens to bar JeansMarines,"* Toronto Globe and Mail, November 11, 2005, A13, http://houstonrunning.blogspot.com/2005/11/marine-corps-marathon-threatens-tobar.html (accessed May 7, 2007). Steve Nearman, "Marathon cheating fiasco raises flags, questions," The Washington Times, March 19, 2006, n.p., http://www.washtimes.com/sports/20060319-011333-1951r.htm (accessed May 7, 2007).

4. *"Canadians cut USMC marathon course,"* LetsRun.com, http:// www.letsrun.com/forum/flat_read.php?thread=1102307 (accessed May 7, 2007). "Jeans Marines? Disgusting," Runner's World, http:// forums. runnersworld.com/eve/forums/a/tpc/f/504106038/m/ 6091049572 (accessed May 7, 2007).

5. Character Unlimited, *"Character, Ethics, Morals and Values...Defined,"* CharacterUnlimited.com, http://www.characterunlimited.com/character_ ethics.htm (accessed May 7, 2007).

6. Michael S. Jones, *"What Is Ethical? Politics, Circumstances, Excuses Can Blur What Is Right,"* ABC News.com (February 21, 2002), cited in Marlene Caroselli, The Business Ethics Activity Book: 50 Exercises for Promoting Integrity at Work (New York: Amacom, 2003), 50.

7. James P. Owen, *Cowboy Ethics: What Wall Street Can Learn from the Code of the West* (Ketchum, Idaho: Stoecklein Publishing, 2004), 71.

8. F. David Peat, "Nature and Ethics," Pari Center for New Learning, http://www.paricenter.com/library/papers/peat23.php (accessed January 1, 2007).

9. University of Miami School of Medicine, *"Ethics Terms and Terminology: A Brief Glossary and Guide to the Ethical 'ISMs',"* Privacy/Data Protection Project, http://privacy.med.miami.edu/glossary/x_ism_guide.htm (accessed December 29, 2006).

10. Norman E. Bowie, *"A Kantian approach to business ethics,"* Companion to Business Ethics, ed. Robert E. Frederick (Malden, MA: Blackwell Publishing, 2002), 9, 12-13.

11. Character Unlimited, *"Character, Ethics."*

12. Ethics Resource Center, *"What is Character Education?,"* Ethics Resource Center, http://www.ethics.org/character-development/character-faqs.asp (accessed January 1, 2007).

13. Mike Thompson, comment on *"Triumph from Tragedy,"* It's All About Character.com, comment posted December 29, 2005, http://www.itsallaboutcharacter.com/php/blogArticle.php?articleID=21 (accessed May 11, 2007).

14. Washington Post, *"Business: Enron,"* Washingtonpost.com, http://www.washingtonpost.com/wp-dyn/business/specials/energy/ enron/(accessed May 11, 2007).

15. Crossroads Programs, *"Corporate Integrity Checkup,"* Crossroads Programs, Inc., http://www.crossroadsprograms.com/corporate.html (accessed January 2, 2007).

16. Rushworth Kidder, *"Ethics and Due Diligence at Cendant: The $14 Billion Moral Collapse,"* Ethics Newsline, August 10, 1998, http://www.globalethics.org/newsline/members/issue.tmpl?articleid=12209914413993 (accessed May 13, 2007).

17. Charles D. Kay, comment on *"Varieties of Egoism,"* Wofford College, comment posted January 20, 1997, http://webs.wofford.edu/kaycd/ethics/egoism.htm (accessed January 1, 2007).

18. University of Miami, *"Ethics Terms."*

19. University of Miami, *"Ethics Terms."*

20. John Collins, *"Why bad things happen to good companies,"* Business Horizons 33, no. 6 (November-December 1990): 18-22.

21. Stephen Parrish, "Review of Viable Values (2004)," review of *Viable Values: A Study of Life as the Root and Reward of Morality,* by Tara

Smith, *The Secular Web*, 2004, http://www.infidels.org/library/modern/ stephen_ parrish/viable-values.shtml (accessed June 14, 2007).

22. Greg Bluestein and Devlin Barrett, *"What was TB guy thinking?,"* The Seattle Times, June 1, 2007, http://seattletimes.nwsource.com/html/ nationworld/2003730475_tb01.html (accessed June 15, 2007).

23. Owen, Cowboy Ethics, 34.

24. Bruce Weinstein, *"Principle No. 3: Respect Others (Part 2),"* Business-Week.com, January 31, 2007, http://www.businessweek.com/careers/ content/jan2007/ca20070131_992542.htm (accessed June 15, 2007).

25. Deon Melchior, *"Things in grey area,"* Articleclick.com, http://www. articleclick.com/grey.html (accessed December 29, 2006).

26. *"Grey area,"* Dictionary.com, WordNet 2.1, Princeton University, http:// dictionary.reference.com/browse/grey area (accessed December 29, 2006).

27. Charles E. Watson, *What Smart People Do When Dumb Things Happen at Work* (New York: Barnes & Noble, 1999), 43.

28. Ray C. Stedman, *"No Gray Areas,"* The Official Ray C. Stedman Library (May 10, 2007), http://www.raystedman.org/power/0510.html (accessed May 13, 2007) (commenting on 1 John 2:20-21).

29. Carl Skooglund and Glenn Coleman, *"Advice from The Ethics Office at Texas Instruments Corporation: Proprietary and Other Sensitive Information,"* onlineethics.org, http://onlineethics.org/corp/infosec.html (accessed May 13, 2007).

30. Leonardo Tondo and Ross J. Baldessarini, *"Suicide: Historical, Descriptive, and Epidemiological Considerations,"* Medscape Today (March 15, 2001), http://www.medscape.com/viewprogram/352 (accessed May 13, 2007).

31. *"Fall of Arthur Anderson,"* Center for Management Research, http:// www.icmr.icfai.org/casestudies/catalogue/Business%20Ethics/ BECG027.htm (accessed June 15, 2007).

32. Roger E. Herman, *Keeping Good People* (New York: McGraw-Hill, 1991), 60, 76.

33. Ralph Waldo Emerson, *The Conduct of Life*, 1860, reprinted at *"Wealth,"* The Works of Ralph Waldo Emerson, http://www.rwe.org/ comm/ index.php?option=com_content&task=view&id=169&Itemid =205 (accessed December 29, 2006).

34. Surfs-Up News, "Bobby Jones," *The Surfs-Up News*, http://www.the-surfs-up.com/sports/bobbyjones.html (accessed May 14, 2007). Greg Feldmeth, "Heinz Ethics in the Workplace Panel Discussion: Ethics in Architecture," Polytechnic School, http://www.polytechnic.org/faculty/gfeldmeth/ethicsmain.html (accessed May 14, 2007).

35. Feldmeth, "Heinz Ethics."

36. Robert J. Rafalko, *"Money, Ethics and the M.B.A.,"* The New York Times, August 23, 2002, letter to editor, http://query.nytimes.com/gst/fullpage.html?res=9F05E6DE153CF930A1575BC0A9649C8B63 (accessed May 14, 2007).

37. MAWIMike, comment on *"When does the end justify the means?,"* Ethics Forum, comment posted April 19, 2007, http://www.ethics.org.au/ethics_forum/forum_posts.asp?TID=2180&PN=1 (accessed May 14, 2007).

38. Robert L. Jolles, *The Way of the Road Warrior: Lessons in Business and Life from the Road Most Traveled* (San Francisco: Jossey-Bass, 2006), 26-27.

39. Harvey Fialkov, *"Ricky Williams fails drug test again,"* Sun-Sentinel.com, May 12, 2007, http://www.sun-sentinel.com/sports/sfl-511williams, 0,4966929.story?coll=sfla-sports-front (accessed May 12, 2007).

40. Carmine Coyote, *"Ends and Means,"* SlowLeadership.org (October 18, 2006), http://www.slowleadership.org/2006/10/ends-and-means.html (accessed May 14, 2007).

41. Debra Gore-Mann, interview by the author, October 9, 2006.

42. Michael David Smith, comment on *"CTA Nominee, Worst Coaching Move: Nick Saban's Lie,"* NFL Fanhouse, comment posted January 31, 2007, http://ctas.aolsportsblog.com/2007/01/31/cta-nominee-worst-coaching-move-nick-sabans-lie/(accessed May 15, 2007).

43. Josiah Royce, *The Philosophy of Loyalty,* 1908, reprint (Nashville, Tennessee: Vanderbilt University Press, 1995), n.p.

44. Lizabeth England, *"Business Ethics,"* Language and Civil Society, http://exchanges.state.gov/Forum/Journal/business.htm (accessed January 1, 2007).

45. Jeff Sutherland, comment on *"Kaizen Mind: Essential to High Performance Scrum Teams,"* Scrum Log Jeff Sutherland, comment posted February 17, 2007, http://jeffsutherland.com/scrum/labels/ toyota%20lean%20kaizen.html (accessed May 15, 2007).

46. Character Unlimited, "Character, Ethics."

47. Lee C. Archie, "Morals, Ethics, and Metaethics," Lander University, http://philosophy.lander.edu/ethics/types.html (accessed December 29, 2006).

48. B. David Brooks, "The Bottom Line on Character," Josephson Institute of Ethics, 2007, http://www.josephsoninstitute.org/business-ethics_ pocdavid-brooks.html (accessed June 15, 2007).

49. Brian Griffiths, Robert A. Sirico, Norman Barry, and Frank Field, *Capitalism, Morality and Markets* (London: The Institute of Economic Affairs, 2001), n.p.

50. *"Word for the Wise," Merriam-Webster.com, January 2, 2007, www.webster.com/cgi-bin/wftwarch.pl?010207 (accessed June 15, 2007).*

51. Ellen Frankel Paul, ed., *"Ethics, Politics, and Human Nature,"* Social Philosophy & Policy 8, no. 1 (Autumn 1990), introduction, http:// www.bgsu.edu/offices/sppc/humnatu.htm (accessed May 14, 2007).

52. T. Y. Okosun, "Business and Ethics = Business Ethics?," Northeastern Illinois University, Chicago, May 15, 2000, http://www.neiu. edu/tokosun/Courses/businessethics.htm (accessed January 1, 2007).

53. Steve Wyche, *"Possible Vick ban a concern to Blank,"* The Atlanta Jour-nal-Constitution, May 11, 2007, sports, http://www.ajc.com/sports/ content/sports/falcons/stories/2007/05/10/0511vickdogs.html (accessed May 15, 2007). Doug Monroe, comment on "Michael Vick and the pit bulls," Atlanta Magazine Online, comment posted May 10, 2007, http://www.atlantamagazine.com/blogs/ entry.php?id=1248 (accessed May 15, 2007).

54. Don Banks, *"A quarterback in trouble: Dog fighting latest example of Vick's bad judgment,"* SI.com, May 10, 2007, http://sportsillustrated.cnn.com/2007/ writers/don_banks/05/09/vick/index.html (accessed May 15, 2007).

55. Wyche, "Blank."

56. Banks, "Quarterback."

57. Sandy Barbour, telephone interview by the author, October 4, 2006.

58. Christopher Bauer, *"A 'Preventive Maintenance' Approach to Ethics,"* The CEO Refresher, 2005, http://www.refresher.com/!crbethics.html (accessed January 1, 2007).

59. Sandy Barbour, telephone interview by the author, October 4, 2006.

60. Marianne M. Jennings and Jon Entine, *"Business With a Soul: A Reexamination of What Counts in Business Ethics,"* Hamline Jounral of Public Law & Policy 20, no. 1 (Fall 1998): n.p., http://www.jonentine.com/articles/business_with_soul.htm (accessed June 15, 2007).

61. Albert Carr, "Is Business Bluffing Ethical?," *Harvard Business Review* 46 (January-February 1968): n.p., located on "James Moulder," Texas A&M University-Corpus Christi, http://falcon.tamucc.edu/~sencerz/Carr_ Business_Bluffing.htm (accessed October 3, 2006).

62. BBC, "IOC may expel more members," *BBC Online Network*, February 10, 1999, http://news.bbc.co.uk/2/hi/sport/276765.stm (accessed May 15, 2007). BBC, "Polishing the Olympic image," *BBC Online Network*, February 10, 1999, http://news.bbc.co.uk/2/hi/sport/276683.stm (accessed May 15, 2007).

63. Cable News Network, "Salt Lake Olympics rocked by resignations, evidence of payments," *CNN.com*, January 8, 1999, http://www.cnn.com/US/9901/08/olympic.bribes.03/(accessed May 15, 2007). BBC, "IOC."

64. BBC, "IOC." BBC, "Polishing."

65. Manuel Velasquez, Claire Andre, Thomas Shanks, and Michael J. Meye, *"Ethical Relativism,"* Issues in Ethics 5, no. 2 (Summer 1992): n.p.

66. Sri Swani Sivananda, *All About Hinduism (Himalayas, India: The Divine Life Society, 1999),* http://www.dlshq.org/download/hinduismbk.htm (accessed January 1, 2007).

67. ThinkExist, *"William Penn quotes,"* ThinkExist.com, http://thinkexist.com/quotation/right_is_right-even_if_everyone_is_against_it-and/180053.html (accessed May 16, 2007).

68. Sandy Barbour, telephone interview by the author, October 4, 2006.

69. Debra Gore-Mann, interview by the author, October 9, 2006.

70. David B. Montgomery and Catherine A. Ramus, "Corporate Social Responsibility Reputation Effects on MBA Job Choice," research paper, Stanford University, 2003, n.p.

71. Amy Corenblith, "Companies Must Vigilantly Tend Reputation, Alsop Says," University of Texas, Austin McCombs School of Business, May 3, 2004, http://www.mccombs.utexas.edu/news/pressreleases/alsop_wrap.asp (accessed May 16, 2007).

72. USA Today, *"Philip Morris changes name to Altria,"* USA Today.com, January 27, 2003, http://www.usatoday.com/money/industries/food/2003-01-27-altria_x.htm (accessed May 15, 2007).

73. *Sourcewatch, "Altria Group,"* SourceWatch.org, May 14, 2007, http://www.sourcewatch.org/index.php?title=Philip_Morris (accessed May 15, 2007).

74. Watson, *Smart People,* 181.

75. MSNBC, *"Airline passengers dissatisfied with service,"* MSNBC.com, May 15, 2007, http://www.msnbc.msn.com/id/18661797/(accessed May 15, 2007). Jena McGregor, Frederick F. Jespersen, and Megan Tucker, *"Customer Service Champs,"* BusinessWeek, March 5, 2007, cover story, http:/ /www.businessweek.com/magazine/content/07_10/ b4024001. htm?chan=rss_ topStories_ssi_5 (accessed May 15, 2007).

76. Lawrence M. Hinman, *Ethics: A Pluralisitc Approach to Ethical Theory,* 3rd ed (Belmont, CA: Wadsworth, 2002), reprinted at *"Glossary,"* Ethics Updates—Glossary, http://ethics.sandiego.edu/LMH/E2/Glossary.asp (accessed January 1, 2007).

77. Auguste Comte, *Catechisme Positiviste* (1852), quoted in Tibor R. Machan, *"Why the Welfare State Is Immoral,"* The Freeman: Ideas on Liberty 41, no. 6 (June 1991): n.p., http://www.fee.org/publications/the-freeman/article.asp?aid=904 (accessed January 1, 2007).

78. John C. Maxwell, *There's No Such Thing as "Business" Ethics: There's Only One Rule for Making Decisions* (New York: Warner Books, 2003), 21.

79. Starbucks Corporation, *"Environmental affairs,"* Starbucks.com, http://www.starbucks.com/aboutus/envaffairs.asp (accessed May 15, 2007).

80. Delta Air Lines, Inc., *"Habitat for Humanity,"* Delta.com, http:// www.delta.com/about_delta/global_good/habitat/index.jsp (accessed May 15, 2007).

81. Character Unlimited, *"Character, Ethics."*

82. Bob Bowlsby, telephone interview by the author, October 4, 2006.

83. Debra Gore-Mann, interview by the author, October 9, 2006.

84. Jayne O'Donnell, *"Whistle-blowers form a breed apart,"* USA Today.com, July 29, 2004, http://www.usatoday.com/money/companies/management/2004-07-29-whistle-blower-main_x.htm (accessed May 15, 2007).

85. Wyeth, *"Mission, Vision and Values,"* Wyeth.com, www.wyeth.com/ aboutwyeth/whoweare/mission (accessed June 15, 2007).

86. Keith Sharp, *"Vengeance,"* Truth Magazine 23, no. 34 (August 31, 1979): n.p., http://truthmagazine.com/archives/volume23/TM023231. htm (accessed January 1, 2007).

87. Maxwell, *"Business"* Ethics, 116-17.

88. Refrigeration Research, "Company Policy," Refrigeration Research, Incorporated, http://www.refresearch.com/policy.html (accessed May 17, 2007).

89. Nicholas N. Kittrie and Eldon D. Wedlock, Jr., eds., *The Tree of Liberty: A Documentary History of Rebellion and Political Crime in America* (Baltimore: The Johns Hopkins University Press, 1998), 157, excerpts reprinted on http://www.thirdworldtraveler.com/History/ Consolidation_Schism_TOL.html (accessed May 17, 2007).

90. William Miller, *"Workplace Discrimination in the European Union,"* International Business Ethics Review 3, no. 1 (February 1, 1999), n.p., http://www.business-ethics.org/newsdetail.asp?newsid=24 (accessed June 15, 2007).

91. Edward B. Nuhfer, *"An Ethical Framework for Practical Reasons,"* The National Teaching & Learning Forum 10, no. 5 (September 2001), n.p.

92. Scott McCartney, *"Business Simulation Tests Ethical Decision-Making,"* WSJ.com, June 1, 2004, http://www.collegejournal.com/mbacenter/ newstrends/20040601-mccartney.html (accessed May 15, 2007).

AFTERWORD

I am a firm believer in continuous improvement. Indeed, I would be the first to admit that I am not a perfect individual. The exercise of researching and writing this book has been an invaluable tool in assisting me and my law firm to enhance our ethical standards and core values. I will continue the journey to achieve the high ethical values I have set for myself and my law firm. I hope you and your organizations will join us in this effort. If so, we can influence how organizations and people in our society treat each other.

The preparation of this book highlighted four important lessons that I have applied in my professional career and personal life, as well as in the ethical standards for my law firm:

- An ethical code must be applied not only to an organization's directors, officers, managers, and employees, but also to its vendors, contractors, suppliers, and stakeholders.
- An organization's decisions, behavior, and activities must be consistent with its code of ethics and values.
- Just because something is legal does not mean it is ethical. Thus, do not take an action if it violates your code of ethics.
- Alleged unethical, questionable, or illicit activity does not warrant an organization or professional to engage in similar behavior.

I look forward to continuing my exploration and discovery in the many theories of ethics. I hope that this book is helpful to you as well.

ABOUT THE AUTHOR

Michael L. Buckner is shareholder of the Michael L. Buckner Law Firm, a boutique investigation law firm. Mr. Buckner, a licensed attorney and private investigator, assists organizations with addressing compliance, investigation, ethics, training, and management enhancement issues.

Mr. Buckner speaks regularly at national and regional conventions, meetings, seminars, and workshops. He also conducts private and public seminars for managers, administrators, attorneys, and other professionals on ethics, leadership, compliance, efficiency, and investigation issues. Further, Mr. Buckner has written numerous articles and reference materials regarding ethics, productivity, compliance, investigation, and operational efficiency issues in national publications and on industry Web sites. Mr. Buckner's first book, *Athletics Investigation Handbook: A Guide for Institutions and Involved Parties During the NCAA Enforcement Process,* was published in August 2004.

Mr. Buckner was formerly with Holland & Knight LLP, one of the largest international law firms. While at the firm, Mr. Buckner headed the collegiate sports administration and compliance practice. He also represented clients in education, commercial, product liability, and appellate legal matters. Mr. Buckner is admitted to practice before the United States Supreme Court, the United States Court of Appeals for the Eleventh Circuit, and all federal and state courts in Florida.

In his community, Mr. Buckner served as a Broward County Commission-appointed member of the Broward County Charter Review Commission from 2006-08 (and chaired the commission's transportation subcommittee). He also is a member of the National Association of College and University Attorneys. He served as an appointed member of the Florida Bar Education Law Committee and the Florida Council for Compulsive Gambling board of directors. From 2000-04, Mr. Buckner served as a governor-appointed commissioner on the non-partisan Volunteer Florida, the Governor's Commission on Volunteerism and Community Service.

Mr. Buckner earned his bachelor's degree in international relations and social sciences and communication in 1993 from the University of Southern

California. He was awarded a law degree in 1996 from Florida State University, where he was a member of the moot court team.

In his personal time, Mr. Buckner enjoys spending time with his wife, Shawn, and two children, as well as cooking, movies, reading, and sports. Mr. Buckner also is an avid runner and regularly travels the country competing in marathons and half-marathons.

Mr. Buckner can be reached via e-mail (info@michaelbucknerlaw.com) or through the law firm website (www.michaelbucknerlaw.com).

REFERENCES

Aristotle. *Nichomachean Ethics.* Translated by W. D. Ross. Oxford: Clarendon Press, 1908.

Behnke, Stephen. *"APA's new Ethics Code from a practitioner's perspective."* Monitor on Psychology 35, no. 4 (April 2004).

Clark, Donald. "Leadership." *Big Dog and Little Dog* (May 15, 2001). http://www.nwlink.com/~donclark/documents/leadership.doc (accessed January 1, 2007).

Craig, H. Kent. "Honesty and Ethics are Profit Centers." *Contractor* (December 2004). http://www.contractormag.com/articles/column.cfm?columnid=358 (accessed January 1, 2007).

CreatingMinds. http://creatingminds.org/index.htm (accessed January 2, 2007).

Djehuty. *"The ethics of selfishness."* Newsvine.com (July 21, 2006). http://djehuty.newsvine.com/_news/2006/07/21/295192-the-ethics-of-selfishness (accessed January 1, 2007).

Gracián y Morales, Baltasar. *The Art of Worldly Wisdom.* Translated by Joseph Jacobs. London: MacMillan and Co., 1892.

Hadzipetros, Peter. *"Playing by the rules."* CBC Sports (November 25, 2005). http://www.cbc.ca/sports/columns/running/rules.html (accessed December 29, 2006).

Harned, Patricia J. *"Why We Do Character Development (and Why It Matters)."* Ethics Today 4, no. 2 (December 21, 2005). http://www.ethics.org/erc-publications/ethics-today.asp?aid=706 (accessed January 1, 2007).

Heathfield, Susan M. "All You Have Is Your Integrity: Why Leave Your Integrity to Chance?" *About.com.* http://humanresources.about. com/ od/businessethics/a/integrity.htm (accessed January 1, 2007).

Johnson, Kenneth W. "Framework for Assessing Ethics/Compliance Programs." Ethics & Policy Integration Centre (1999). http://www. ethicaledge.com/ assessment%20framework.htm (accessed January 1, 2007).

Josephson Institute of Ethics, The. "Resources-Quote Library: Quote Unquote." Character Counts! http://www.josephsoninstitute.org/quotes/ quotetoc.htm (accessed January 1, 2007).

Kroeker, Wally. *"A Hiding Place Of Gray."* InterVarsity's Ministry in Daily Life Resource Group (October 17, 2004). http://www.ivmdl. org/godsweek. cfm?article=42 (accessed January 1, 2007).

LaPlante, Alice. *"MBA Graduates Want to Work for Caring and Ethical Employers."* Stanford University Graduate School of Business (January 2004). http://www.gsb.stanford.edu/news/research/hr_mbajobchoice. shtml (accessed January 1, 2007).

Machan, Tibor R. *"Business Ethics in a Free Society."* Blackwell Companion to Business Ethics. Oxford: Blackwell, 1999. Quoted in Suyash R. Rai. *"Social Responsibility of Business Organizations—The role of managers."* Terra Firma. eds. Shahid Ahmad Khan and K. Somanadha Babu. Gujarat, India: Institute of Rural Management Anand, 2006.

Murphy, Liam B. *"The Demands of Beneficence."* Philosophy and Public Affairs 22, no. 4 (Autumn 1993).

Nepfel, Bill. *Interview by the author,* October 9, 2006.

Online Ethics Center Glossary, The. http://onlineethics.org/glossary. html#anchT (accessed January 2, 2007).

QuoteDB. http://www.quotedb.com (accessed January 2, 2007).

Quotations Page, The. http://www.quotationspage.com (accessed January 2, 2007).

Quotionary. ed. Leonard Roy Frank. New York: Random House, 2001.

Sahadi, Jeanne. "When good executives do bad things." *CNN Money* (October 2, 2006). http://money.cnn.com/2006/10/02/commentary/sahadi/ ?postversion=2006100213 (accessed January 1, 2007).

"Values and Ethics." *Strategic Leadership and Decision Making (2002)*. http:// www.au.af.mil/au/awc/awcgate/ndu/strat-ldr-dm/pt4ch15.html (accessed January 1, 2007).

Watton Pentecostal Church. *"What the Bible has to say."* Watton on the Web. http://www.watton.org/ethics/bible/index.html#john_13_34.htm (accessed January 1, 2007).

"Welcome!" New York State Ethics Commission. http://www.dos.state.ny.us/ethc/ethics.html (accessed January 2, 2007).

Wisdom Quotes. http://www.wisdomquotes.com (accessed January 2, 2007).

Yehuda Berg's Blog (May 30, 2004-June 5, 2004). http://blog.kabbalah.com/ yehuda/2004/05/28/finish-what-you-start/en/(accessed January 1, 2007).

"Zero Tolerance." *Lockheed Martin Today*. Reprint, United States Department of the Air Force Office of the General Counsel. http://www.safgc.hq.af.mil/ docs/sas_lm_article.pdf (accessed January 1, 2007).

LaVergne, TN USA
03 March 2010
174723LV00004B/10/P

9 781935 278498